Dress in the Middle Ages

Dress in the Middle Ages

Françoise Piponnier and Perrine Mane

Translated by Caroline Beamish

Yale University Press
New Haven and London

Designed by Laura Church
Typeset by SX Composing DTP, Rayleigh, Essex
Printed and bound in Great Britain by
Biddles Ltd, Guildford and Kings Lynn

Library of Congress Cataloging-in-Publication Data

Piponnier, Françoise.
[Se vêtir au Moyen Âge.   English]
Dress in the Middle Ages/Françoise Piponnier, Perrine Mane;
translated by Caroline Beamish.
p.   cm.
Includes bibliographical references and index.
ISBN 0-300-08691-1
1. Costume–History–Medieval, 500–1500.   2. Costume in art.
3. Civilization, Medieval.   I. Mane, Perrine.   II. Title.
GT575.P5613
391' .0094' 0902–DC21   96–29994
CIP

A catalogue record for this book is available from
The British Library

Contents

Foreword

ALTHOUGH PROTECTING ONE'S BODY from the elements is among mankind's most basic needs, clothing has not attracted the attention of social historians to the same extent as have food and housing. Nevertheless, in recent years more research has been devoted to the subject, different kinds of question have been asked and new techniques of analysis been employed, particularly in relation to the medieval period. This book aims to present some of this knowledge to the general reader.

Omitting the very earliest periods, we have confined ourselves to a relatively short span of the Middle Ages, depending on the type of documentary evidence. It is not until the Carolingian period that illustrated documents, texts and archaeological data exist in sufficient quantity for their collation to provide a clear indication of overall developments.

We obviously had to ignore twentieth-century national and linguistic boundaries, meaningless for the medieval era, and have placed our study within the cultural boundaries of the period: the Latin world of the West was bordered to the south by the Islamic world and, on its eastern edges, by the Byzantine sphere of influence. Our own linguistic limitations and the inaccessibility of translated editions of certain manuscripts have led to some omissions and have prevented our straying as far as we would have liked across these boundaries.

It has not been possible in a book of this length to do justice to all aspects of recent research. Our inclination has been to concentrate on the most original findings to have emerged from recent studies of medieval modes of dress: important economic differentials, strongly coded social discriminants and, last but not least, modes of expression open to many different interpretations.

Part One

Approaches to Medieval Costume

CHAPTER ONE

Sources and Applications

TRUE OR FALSE? ART AS WITNESS TO AN AGE

At first glance it might appear that clothed figures abound in medieval art: men and women are captured in stone around the doorways of cathedrals, or hidden away between the parchment leaves of gold, purple and sky-blue miniature paintings.

It is in terms of quantity that the main variations between periods and regions manifest themselves. Some materials, in particular textiles and wood, are fragile; only a few exceptional examples have survived, such as the eleventh-century embroidery known as the Bayeux Tapestry, and some later embroideries and painted fabrics. Tastes also change: from the Middle Ages on, Romanesque buildings with their painted and carved decoration began to be demolished to make way for Gothic cathedrals. By the seventeenth and eighteenth centuries medieval art was itself in disfavour, and more than one cathedral was disfigured with neo-classical plasterwork, its stained glass being removed and replaced by colourless windows. Medieval abbeys, secular buildings, objects and hangings suffered even greater damage.

Notwithstanding current efforts to preserve the basic essentials, the twentieth century has taken its toll: wars, in particular the Second World War, have swept across almost the whole of what was the medieval western world, taking with them a great deal of the evidence that had hitherto survived.

Regional differences are responsible for imposing further limitations on iconographic evidence. Artistic expression took different forms at differents times across Europe and was not to be found in equal measure everywhere. Production depended on patronage and reflected the demand and the ideology of the patron. Civil authority, after the intense centralisation of the Carolingian Empire, became somewhat diluted. The Church continued to commission elaborate pieces of work to decorate buildings and to accompany acts of worship, but in the monastic world a brake was put on decoration by the

1   Lorenzo and Jacopo Salimbeni: *Baptism of Christ* (detail).
Oratorio San Giovanni Battista, Urbino, fresco, 1416. Loose
overgarments, open under the arms, were worn by male
members of the aristocracy in fifteenth-century Florence.

influence of the Cistercians, who rejected all ornamentation in their
bare-walled architecture. The growth of towns and the formation of
kingdoms, with the concomitant economic development and con-
centration of wealth, stimulated the emergence of a less exclusively
religious art, and one that varied from region to region. Although this
development persisted to the end of the Middle Ages, modes of
expression and artistic centres changed.

Even when art was created for the laity it remained devotional in
inspiration throughout the whole of the Middle Ages. The principal
objective of any work of art, whether it was a huge architectural
scheme or a small object for personal devotion, was to illustrate and
propagate the precepts of Christianity. An artist depicting characters

from the Bible or the lives of the best-loved saints would often copy earlier representations, without bringing the clothing up-to-date. Or he might take his inspiration from his own surroundings, dressing his figures according to the custom of the day. Scenes from the Bible, or representations of the seasons in which each month of the year is symbolised by an activity, gave the artist scope to depict everyday reality. Religious subjects, however, were not treated in realistic fashion until the fourteenth century, when secular art began to develop separately. Copies of earlier models and stereotypes did not disappear altogether, largely because there were still workshops mass-producing them.

Pictorial representation cannot therefore be used as the only reliable source for the study of medieval costume. Each item has to be viewed strictly in the context of its production, and its documentary value be considered in the light of the author's intentions and the techniques employed. It is often difficult to date works with any certitude. For example, a funeral effigy on a stone slab may bear the date of its subject's death, yet it may have been executed decades later and may represent the deceased wearing clothes or armour that he never wore in his lifetime.

The dimensions of a piece of work also have some bearing on the information to be gathered from it, although once again this cannot be relied upon totally. The quality of workmanship and the care in handling details varied, even in the work of the most skilled artists. Sculpture has the advantage of representing three-dimensional figures, generally on quite a large scale. Clothes, with their draperies and their accessories, are often rendered very faithfully, even though the colours may have faded or been altered by weather or by restoration. The small size of ivories, enamels and medals, and even more so of the wax or lead seals attached to documents on parchment, necessitated the simplification of forms. The constraint inherent in media such as mosaic, stained glass or embroidery imposed a degree of stylisation that did not favour detailed representation of styles of clothing. These techniques, however, provide important information about colour, itself one of the key elements of costume. Painting is also irreplaceable in this respect, although the possibility of changes to the colours used by artists on wooden panels or on fabrics has to be borne in mind. Miniature paintings have in general been better protected from the ravages of time. Still on the subject of colour, we are faced with the problem of whether these reflect contemporary reality with any exactitude. In fact the range of colours used was often

2   *Meditationes Vitae Christi.* Bibliothèque Nationale, Paris, It. 115, f.8v, illuminated in Siena *c.*1330–40. The Virgin Mary is handing out loaves of bread to the
poor, one of whom is dressed in a fur mantle of modest quality, worn with the
fur outside.

limited by technical constraints; in the oldest frescoes the tones are
muted and there is no evidence of the use of blue or bright red.
Miniatures, on the other hand, retain their sparkling colours, in particular those painted in the late Middle Ages; the brilliance of the
richest of these is enhanced with gold. Furthermore, the artists'
choice and combination of colours carry meanings that have to be
decoded individually: some colours exalt the person wearing them,
others demonstrate the wearer's lack of prestige or even vices.

To add to these difficulties, it must be remembered that pictorial
representations do not give us the kind of panorama of medieval society in which the various social groups would be represented in proportion to their numbers. Like the Church, medieval iconography is
predominantly masculine. Members of the female orders seldom
appear at the side of the popes and bishops, priests and monks. Female
figures are scarce among the laity as well, and are seldom depicted
until late in the Middle Ages. Neither women nor children are to be
found in the carved stone representations of the seasons of the twelfth
and thirteenth centuries. In giving importance to the great and
powerful, these reflect the hierarchical society in which they were
made. A pope, bishop or abbot will take precedence over a simple

priest or monk, unless the priest or monk has been canonised. Emperors, kings and powerful landowners and, at a later date, well-to-do city dwellers impose their presence; the overwhelming majority of the population, the peasants and small townsfolk, lurk in the shadows to emerge only at the dawn of the modern era. Medieval representation cannot therefore be considered as documentation to be used as it stands; by a series of comparisons and contrasts, however, it is possible to eliminate certain stereotypes, including simplified or encoded images, and to arrive at an approximate chronology; other sources are of enormous assistance to this approach.

From Romance to Account Book

Although written texts have for many years been regarded as the most reliable historical source, they have been used only infrequently in conjunction with figurative records; written documents have proved invaluable in the dating of pictorial evidence, and for the identification of its context as well. The majority of texts, however, bear no relation to images or objects; only in exceptional cases is their main aim to describe clothes, the way they were worn and what was worn with what. In each of these cases the author's intentions need careful analysis so that the validity of the description can be assessed.

Literary texts, such as romances, epics and lyric poetry, generally idealise their heroes or heroines; to make the reader dream they ascribe to the hero or heroine, in addition to perfect beauty, all the stereotypical details of princely raiment or, at the other extreme, paint a gloomy picture of a hideous, dirty peasant wearing animal skins which reduce him to the level of a brute beast. Chroniclers and historians select the facts that they record, sometimes distorting reality in their eagerness to extol the reigning sovereign or their own party. Here and there, however, scenes drawn from life throw light on contemporary attitudes to dress: by setting himself up as a censor, the author reveals various aspects of the ruling proprieties. Moralising clerics rail in their sermons against the developments of fashion, condemning them for inciting loose morals and singling them out as symptomatic of the moral decay of society. These sketches, often highly exaggerated, give more information about the wilder innovations of fashion than about everyday dress and its use.

Regulations and sumptuary laws were adopted for reasons more complex than simply the control of excess in dress. Their aim was sometimes to limit the importing of expensive raw materials, or to prevent members of the aristocracy from facing financial ruin because of excessive spending on clothing. More frequently their aim was to prevent newly rich members of the bourgeoisie from trying to out-shine the aristocracy and, among the aristocracy, to control feminine over-indulgence on clothes. Some of the regulations were drawn up to stigmatise groups for their religious adherence (Jews and heretics), or to protect public morals (prostitutes). The decrees sometimes went into great detail about raw materials, fabric and furs, price, colour and the accessories to be worn, but like all regulations the sumptuary laws represented a desired state of affairs rather than one that was ever achieved, since they were endlessly reiterated. The fact that, from the thirteenth century onwards, the authorities should have attempted to control peoples' appearance underlines the importance that clothing had begun to assume as a mark of the status of the individual, even in the eyes of the authorities.

Other archival documents give further information about the way individuals chose to dress: account books, inventories and, to a lesser extent, wills and testaments were all used in the management of material possessions. The intrinsic value of clothing was high in the Middle Ages and, as a result, items of clothing were listed individu-ally, sometimes with a detailed description and an estimate of their value, when they were acquired or sold on. Although these docu-ments were not common until quite late in the period (the thirteenth and fourteenth centuries or even the fifteenth) and did not cover the whole of Europe, they reveal information about costume which is solidly rooted in fact. The richest sources are the ledgers of kings, princes and (less frequently) rich bourgeois, in which mention is made of the materials and processes used in the production of each item of clothing; the cost of each garment and its recipient is also noted. All the members of a court, or an entire middle-class family, can be reconstructed from this information; differences of age and sta-tus are signalled by the quality, quantity, colour and ornamentation of the clothes attributed to each person, and the frequency with which each wardrobe was renewed can also be judged.

Inventories of property offer a more static picture. They were usually drawn up when someone died and list the wardrobe of the deceased, or at least the items not yet distributed as charity or bequests. Even though each entry is briefer than it would be in a book of accounts, the most complete inventories set the clothes owned at a given time by an individual in a precise geographical, economic and social context. The personal cirumstances revealed in these documents are extremely varied. Inventories of personal possessions have been left by urban artisans, a few servants (male and female) and manual labourers. Because of their legal status as servants some peasants, including the very poverty-stricken, and even beggars, had their property inventoried and then auctioned off to the benefit of their employer.

The most commonly found document is the last will and testament, examples of which pre-date inventories; the most deprived social classes are not represented, however, because in order to write a will an individual had to have owned at least a few possessions. In addition to standardised bequests, such as a wedding dress left to a spinster daughter or a precious piece of fabric used as a funeral pall before being donated to the church, various more personal attributions appear: the best gowns owned by the deceased are left to the children or godchildren, or to a serving maid. Occasionally a peasant will leave his whole wardrobe to members of his household. Information about clothing, its manufacture and materials can be found in other types of archival document, but as these details are so widely dispersed, they are difficult to collate and classify.

ARCHAEOLOGY, THE MATERIAL EVIDENCE

The few garments that survive from the Middle Ages are also widely dispersed, yet the information that they yield is invaluable. Even quite ordinary fabric was expensive and represented a considerable outlay at the time, and it seems likely that clothes were worn until they were worn out, possibly by a succession of wearers, and that the parts that were still usable were re-used in different ways. Apart from royal suits of clothing, the most famous of which belonged to the German emperors, having been inherited from the Norman kings of Sicily, most of the surviving pieces were preserved as relics in memory of a saint or of someone whose relations hoped to see him beatified. Some of these pieces have been securely identified and dated, but the coronation robe of Roger II, King of Sicily (now in the Schatzkammer in Vienna), which has its date and place of fabrication woven into the selvedge (Palermo, 1133), remains an exception. In quite a number

3   The Chelles
Reliquary: purse
decorated with
scenes from courtly
life. Musée de
Chelles, 1170–80.
The few surviving
examples of medieval
textiles give valuable
information about
embroidery tech-
niques and about
braids and bindings.

of cases the traditional attribution has had to be revised after scientific analysis. Moreover it is not certain whether or not the garments have been preserved in their original form. Liturgical garments were some-time restyled to suit the fashion of the day, and civilian clothing was even more liable to be altered. There is certainly much more still to be discovered in the treasuries of cathedrals and churches or inside reliquaries and shrines. As far as armour is concerned, most of the suits of armour to be found in museums date from the late Middle Ages and their numbers have been reduced since recent more critical examination weeded out some fakes and some improper reconstruc-tions. The authentic pieces mainly come from royal armouries and do not accurately represent the equipment of a medieval warrior. Coats of mail are more frequent, as are suits of ceremonial armour designed for jousting and tournaments. The oldest and commonest styles have not survived because the metal studs fixed to a leather tunic were easy to remove and return to the forge.

The finding of new information depends on the continuing devel-opment of medieval archaeology. Unfortunately, from the earliest days of Christianity, clothed burial was considered a pagan custom. Although it was eschewed for the majority, however, it was tolerated for the great, whether lay or clerical; their tombs are generally situ-ated in churches or monasteries. In cases where conditions for the preservation of organic remains were favourable, excavation of these tombs reveals how the different items of dress were worn together. The single tomb of the Princes of Castille not to have been ransacked by Napoleon's troops, in the monastery of Las Huelgas near Burgos, is a case in point. Here a complete outfit was found, from the shoes to the headdress, in an admirable state of preservation; it had belonged to the Infante Fernando de la Cerda, a known historical figure whose death in 1211 is securely documented. Flimsier evidence often has to suffice: bits of rag or strips of cloth elicit more doubtful reconstructions. Towards the end of the Middle Ages the precepts of the Church were interpreted more loosely and a number of graveyards have yielded vestiges of clothing, in particular leather and metallic remains. Only one graveyard so far has yielded gowns and hoods of coarse wool, the Greenland village of Herjolfsnes, which was occupied in the fourteenth century by a population of Scandinavian origin. Occasionally, after a battle, some of the victims would be tossed into a common grave without being undressed; this was the case at Visby, on the Swedish island of Gotland, where archaeologists have unearthed armaments that can be precisely dated to 1361.

Excavations of early inhabited sites, particularly in towns where the medieval archaeology is protected by thick layers of stratification, have contributed enormously to increasing our knowledge. Although their products are more difficult to interpret than material from burial grounds (because they are generally less well preserved) they have the advantage of being more numerous and more diverse. Because leather can withstand damp conditions, shoes have been recovered in great quantity. The patched boots of ordinary people and the cutwork shoes and painted pattens of the aristocracy share the same grave. Vegetable fibres, unlike wool and especially silk, rarely survive burial. In London the banks of the Thames and wells on other sites have yielded hoods and hose, caps and hats, and fragments of garments large enough to allow the reconstruction of a robe or gown, as well as innumerable scraps of fabric and ribbon. No other source has given so much information about raw materials, techniques of spinning and weaving, dyes and methods of cutting and stitching. When soils have been too well ventilated to favour the preservation of organic materials, the metallic accessories still remain. Museum collections usually display only the most elaborate of these finds, with the result that the more ordinary items have until recently remained virtually unknown. Silver or bronze fibulas, buttons and buckles and other belt ornaments often reproduce the forms of more costly models. The evolution of forms permits the historian to trace the spread of fashion and to chart the passage of different types of ornament from one social class to another.

If we want to understand the relationship between the types of garment worn in the Middle Ages and the meaning accorded to each type by its contemporaries, it is not sufficient to analyse images, documents and objects separately. Evaluation of the authenticity of the various sources is, however, a necessary stage in the process. To reconstruct the costume of men, women, children and old people of the entire medieval West, in all its diversity, is obviously an impossible task, but close examination of the available sources opens new areas of study.

The synthesis of the knowledge contributed by all the different sources is no easy task. However detailed a text may be, it remains difficult to relate the written word to the *realia* supplied by archaeology or the images of iconography. Latin and the vernacular languages use different names to designate the same object and regional variants accompany fabrics, fur and fashions across national boundaries. Language has a tendency to develop at its own pace. One term often persists while the shape of the garment or its length changes; technical progress in the art of dyeing meant that shade or depth of colour might alter.

There are, however, methods of establishing links between the medieval fabrics or garments that remain, and accurate terminology. Samples of fabric attached to a few extremely rare and valuable commercial documents give specific details about the type of fabric and its colour. The scientific analysis of fabrics, in conjunction with often very detailed trade regulations, comes some way towards sorting out the minefield of fabric names and descriptions of colours. Archaeological samples allow the nature and quality of the fibres to be examined and methods of spinning, weaving and dyeing to be assessed; laboratory experiments have proved particularly useful in completing the information that we already have, particularly with regard to amounts used and methods of applying the dyes.

The identification of raw materials from representations is a relatively simple matter as far as furs and decorated silks are concerned, provided that the illustrations are in colour and of large enough size. Even when they are large, however, it is difficult to distinguish silk from wool except by pattern: wool fabrics were suitable only for geometrical forms, stripes or checks, whereas silk-weaving looms made a variety of patterns available. Even cotton cloth, when dyed, is hard to distinguish from plain wool or silk. Finally, although sculpture can convey the appearance of miniver and other furs, or the pattern on a fabric, it is hazardous to try and identify a piece of material that the artist himself may not have attempted to represent in a particularly realistic fashion simply by its fall or by the way pleats or folds are depicted.

In the case of liturgical garments, it is easy to connect medieval terms with the garments that have survived because the names have not changed since the Middle Ages. Civilian clothing is a different matter, as is shown by the hesitation over what to call the famous 'pourpoint' preserved in Lyons (Musée historique des tissus). Close study of princely account books, with their details of materials, measurements, accessories and tailoring, allows one to match technical characteristics with a given designation. A number of attempts have been made to compare documents of an identical date and from the same regions, with encouraging results. Extreme caution is necessary, however, if erroneous identifications are to be avoided. One of the most famous examples is the word 'hennin', applied to the tall pointed hats worn by women at the beginning of the fifteenth century and used on the strength of a much later commentary, at several removes from the original. It appears that a preacher, who was a member of an order particularly opposed to women's interest in personal adornment, promised indulgences to children who would help him in his mission by shouting 'Au hennin!' at any woman wearing such headgear. His invective was taken to be the actual name of the hat.

In spite of gaps and problems of interpretation, surviving sources, especially after the thirteenth century, give a complete enough picture for us to have at least a glimpse of the diversity and contrasts of medieval costume.

Chapter Two

Materials

Throughout the Middle Ages wool was the prime fabric for clothing, but its quality must have varied according to whether the garments were designed for princes or peasants. Moreover, the appearance of woollen fabrics was continually being improved by advances in weaving technology; the trade was thriving, and wool production, re-organised along new lines, saw to it that the technical improvements were widely diffused.

Wool and Colours

Current information about textiles of the high Middle Ages and the Carolingian period is based principally on the study of fragments unearthed during archaeological excavation in northern and eastern Europe. From these finds, experts have been able to deduce that weavers used vertical looms with the warp (and the right side of the fabric) facing them as they worked. Although the length of the fabrics that could be produced in this way was limited, it was possible to produce complex patterns; the textiles of the period bear characteristic diamond and chevron patterns. Documentation is so scarce that little is known about the processes by which these fabrics were produced. It appears that workshops with skilled female weavers were established on large estates in the western countries, where wool from flocks that grazed the land between cultivated areas was woven.

Later, commercial documents attest to the distinctions established by merchants between the different qualities of wool produced for different purposes and sold at widely differing prices. The wools used and the types of sheep reared have been identified by analysis of fibres from the ancient fragments. While the coarser woollen fabrics were still made from the fleece of a sheep known since the Iron Age, other fabrics demonstrate the development of superior, finer wools with a longer staple. The cool, damp, rainy climate of England is often cited

4   Boccaccio: *De claris mulieribus*. New York Public
Library, Spencer Collection 33, f.56, illuminated in France
c.1470. Women carding and spinning wool.

to explain the quality of English wool, clipped from sheep reared on
grazing that abounds throughout the year. The skill of the shepherds
must also have played a part, as it was they who selected the best rams
and picked out good fleeces, thus contributing to the fame of English
wool, particularly that sold by the great Cistercian abbeys in the
northern counties. The production of wool in the Mediterranean
region was stimulated by the eventual disappearance of English wool
from the main continental centres once the local weaving trade had
developed. Certainly from the fifteenth century onwards, in the lands
owned by the royal house of Aragon, exceptionally fine woollen fabrics were produced, resembling those on which the reputation of the
merino breed came to be built.

   The introduction of the horizontal loom caused enormous disrup-
tion to established weaving techniques, but little technical or economic information about the changes remains from the period, when
written texts were few and far between. Historians are in agreement,

however, about ascribing this innovation to the eleventh century and
to western Europe; it is generally considered to be the most important
change to have taken place in textile manufacture in the Middle Ages.
The earliest references to scarlet come from the same time and area.
Scarlet was a luxury fabric characterised by the processes employed to
finish it (fulling [scouring and beating], teasing and clipping were
aimed at giving it the felted and very smooth appearance), but, above
all, by the use of the most expensive dye available, extracted from a
Mediterranean insect, the kermes. The vivid variety of reds gave these
scarlets the same status as was held by the colour purple in Roman
times, and they were reserved for the élite. The towns that specialised
in the preparation and weaving of wool launched an increasing volume
of more everyday woollen fabrics on to the market – via stalls at markets and fairs. The regulations imposed by town councils on members
of the weaving trade, aimed at ensuring sustained high quality, were
not codified until a later date, but it is safe to assume that the processes
described in them were based on the practice of centuries. For the best
quality cloth, careful grading and washing of wool would be followed
by carding, which isolated the longest fibres; spinning by hand, with a
distaff, was preferred to spinning with a wheel right up to the fifteenth
century. The horizontal loom, worked by two weavers, made it possible to produce pieces of fabric measuring as much as thirty metres
long by about two metres wide. Fulling, initially carried out by labourers trampling the cloth in vats of hot water with added substances to
encourage shrinkage and felting of the fabric, was gradually taken over
by machinery. Hydraulic mills or beaters became more common, with
foot fulling reserved for the better quality fabrics, whose width would
be reduced to about a metre and a half by the process.

Perhaps the most important of the finishes that gave woollen cloth
its final appearance was the dyeing. Kermes was extremely expensive
and produced a huge range of colours including 'sanguine' or blood
red; it was the favourite but was reserved for the luxury end of the
market, which spread as far as the eastern and southern shores of the
Mediterranean. Woad cost less because it was extracted from a plant
that could be grown in a number of different regions. Woad dyed
cloth blue or, if combined with other colourings, green; it was con-
venient to use because it needed no mordant and could be used either
for whole fleeces or for ready-spun wool. According to the concen-
tration in which it was used it could give very deep blues or a much
paler shade. Although the richest, darkest colours were still only

5   Barthélemy L'Anglais: *Livre des propriétés des choses*. British
Library, London, Royal 15 E III, f.269, illuminated in Lille *c.*
1482. Dyeing woollen cloth: kermes, a very expensive dye,
produced a range of reds used only on woollen cloth of the
highest quality. Woad, much less expensive, produced blue or,
in combination with other dyestuffs, green.

within the grasp of a minority, this development made coloured fabrics available to an ever-increasing number of people from less exalted
social classes. Blue garments were already quite common among city-
dwellers in the thirteenth century and were beginning to spread to the
countryside by the fourteenth; even quite humble peasants would possess a coloured gown, though its colour might be faded by age and use,
or by the mediocre quality of the dye used on inexpensive woollen
cloth. The better-off peasants had access to a wide range of colours
from now on. The art of dyeing progressed in leaps and bounds during
the last couple of centuries of the Middle Ages; many more substances
were used for colouring – vegetable, animal and mineral, local or
imported. Colours became more diverse and saturation by the dyes
improved, producing the deep shades so popular in the late Middle
Ages: dark greens and blues, violet and especially black.

In written documents the most frequent references to fabrics are to those of high quality. Trade regulations describe the stages in their production in preference to those of the cheaper woollen goods, and commercial documents usually relate to transactions involving expensive fabrics. Descriptions of the stock held by cloth merchants, or testaments and inventories of ordinary folk that might allude to middle-range textiles, are extremely scarce before the closing years of the Middle Ages. It is impossible to be sure that fabrics of equal width are being compared, but the very wide price range implies that there were great differences in quality between the scarlets and the other coloured woollens, and between the various categories of coloured woollens as well.

Another type of woollen fabric, serge, which has a faint diagonal stripe on the surface, was in general use throughout the period. Textiles found in archaeological excavations show the wide variety of fabrics obtained by this method of weaving, from thick, rough cloth for the working classes to delicate fabrics almost as fine as silk. Camelin, tiretaine and, right at the bottom of the price range, 'beige' and 'bureau' were medium-quality fabrics that may sometimes have been woven from wool mixed with other fibres. They appear in large quantity in the inventories of cloth merchants specialising in the the most everyday products and some of the secondary weaving centres made them their speciality. There is no indication in the surviving documents of any manufacture for domestic use, and where weaving developed in the rural areas in the fifteenth century it was always under the impetus of urban entrepreneurs who were looking for cheap labour to reduce the cost of the fabrics they produced.

Spun wool was used for clothing in various ways besides being made into cloth. Two knitting techniques have been identified, one using a single needle in a method resembling netting, the other using two or more needles. Haberdashers or mercers sold clothing made with the needle – children's socks and bootees, nightcaps. The technique was developed particularly for making the felt caps and hats which were a popular feature of male attire from the fifteenth century onwards. Very few knitted garments have survived, probably because they were worn until they were completely worn out. Medieval knitting techniques can be studied, however, through the liturgical gloves and hose of knitted silk carefully preserved in the treasuries of churches and cathedrals.

6   Rogier Van Der Weyden: *Saint Mary Magdalen Reading* (detail). National Gallery, London, 1435–40. Mary Magdalen is dressed in a green wool gown (*houppelande*) lined with grey fur and worn over a *cotte* of cloth of gold. Her head is covered by a white linen veil (with a fluted edge).

Silk from the East, Silk from the West

For a long time silk was so prestigious a textile in the medieval Western world that it was reserved for religious ceremonies, or for decorating churches and cathedrals. The silks of the Far East and of Persia were known and valued in Ancient Rome, and were evidently worn by dignitaries of the Roman Empire. When the Empire collapsed, contact with the East continued via the Byzantine world. The *basileus* tried to hold on the monopoly of both production and export, but Islamic invaders brought oriental technology westwards, introducing the cultivation of silkworms into Sicily and Spain, where local rulers set up workshops in their palaces. Silk production developed and spread in the wake of these conquests. From the thirteenth century onwards, Spain and Italy exported their silks, and competed successfully with Byzantium. Following the Byzantine and Islamic influence on Sicily, the Italian silk trade began to develop in Palermo, moving subsequently up to Amalfi, then to Lucca and finally to Florence, Venice and Genoa. Attempts to introduce silk weaving to the kingdom of France were to no avail until the end of the fifteenth century.

The early, richly brocaded silks were at the outset luxury products that probably figured more frequently as gifts between reigning monarchs than as objects of commerce; they were often embroidered with strips of precious metal and dyed with the costliest dye, the purple whose secret Byzantium had inherited from the Classical world. These silks were used to decorate palaces and were particularly favoured as offerings to churches, where they were used as hangings or for ecclesiastical dress. Silk production began gradually to turn away from such opulence, and although the silk was still brocaded the patterns began to be picked out in contrasting colours rather than in gold. Well before Byzantium had fallen, Spain, and most significantly of all Italy, began to flood the Western market with their silks. Spain produced 'draps d'arest' heavily influenced by the Islamic tradition and other brightly contrasting fabrics. Having broken away from the Byzantine tradition, the Italians created their own repertoire of patterns of all sizes; their mastery of the art of dyeing, at which particularly the Florentines excelled, gave brilliance to the colours of these fabrics. Their brocaded crimson velvets and satins, dyed with cochineal, fetched astronomical prices. After the end of the fourteenth century deep black became the fashion, the silks being dipped repeatedly in a series of dye-baths in which woad and indigo predominated.

As well as producing these sumptuous brocaded silks, Italian weavers began to produce lighter fabrics in plain colours which cost less to buy. Plain samite had the appearance of satin. The least costly of the woven silks was taffeta (first called 'cendal'), which was often used to line silk or woollen garments or to make accessories and cushions.

Silk was distributed most widely in the form of ribbons and braid. As early as the high Middle Ages weaving from patterns made possible the production of elaborately patterned ribbons as borders or for belts or girdles. Archaeological studies of the contents of the tombs of the upper classes prove that silk was one of the materials in most frequent use. At the end of the Middle Ages the fashion for highly

7 Nicolas Haberschrack: *Polyptych of the Augustinians. Adoration of the Magi* (detail). National Museum, Cracow, painted in Poland in 1468. The *houppelandes* worn by the Three Kings are made of silk brocade with fur or orfreys of gold.

ornamented waistbands used these braids to their fullest advantage; gold and silver threads were often interwoven with the silk.

While used widely in the countries where it was produced, silk was much less common north of the Alps and the Pyrenees. In the thirteenth century silken fabrics were reserved for kings and princes, and worn only in exceptional circumstances. They became a little more widespread in the fourteenth century but did not supplant woollen fabrics; they were generally used only in court circles, if not only by princes. It was not until the second half of the fifteenth century that silk came into regular use by royalty, extending to the upper bourgeoisie to such a degree that the urban and court authorities tried to limit its use by tabling regulations restricting the use of this select fabric to the nobility.

VEGETABLE FIBRES

Information about textiles made from such vegetable fibres as linen, hemp or cotton is scarce and belongs to a later date. Archaeology cannot in this instance compensate for the inadequacy of written records because vegetable fibres do not survive well when buried in the ground. When the texts are explicit in their reference to textiles, it is clear that dealing with vegetable fibres was confined to a domestic level. In northern and western Europe where the cool, damp climate favoured its growth, linen (hemp in other areas) was grown by peasants on part of their plot of land. Not only in the country but in town houses there was equipment for preparing and spinning fibres; household inventories often contain details of stocks of such fibres at all stages of preparation and of various qualities. Linen weavers, often women, worked to order, on simple, inexpensive looms, weaving fabric from fibre that remained the property of the person who had spun it or bought it in skeins. They also wove for merchants, but for the most part linen was produced outside the realms of commerce and therefore it evaded the written word. It is mainly thanks to purchases made by the aristocracy that regions where weaving of high quality linens attained almost industrial level can be identified: Flanders, the area around Cambrai, Brittany and above all Holland and Germany, with linen from Konstanz.

Linen was not used simply for undergarments: it was made into short shirts and *braies* for men and long shifts for women. Once babies had emerged from their woollen swaddling clothes lined with linen, they would often be clothed in short linen dresses that were easy to look after. For adults, linen was chiefly used for headdresses. The close-fitting coifs or 'cauls' worn in the thirteenth century by men from every milieu, including the highest social class, persisted until the fifteenth century in working-class dress. Throughout the Western world women wore linen veils, draped and decorated according to local fashion. Although frequently outshone in contemporary iconography by the sumptuous finery of the noblewomen or the chaperons of the bourgeoisie, coifs made of fine or coarse linen were the commonest daytime headwear for women and were worn at night by men and women alike.

Coarser linen was used to make the smocks and pinafores worn as protection for the clothes underneath; these were not however very widely used. There is evidence that linen was waxed to make it

8 Calendar. Notre-Dame, Pritz, fresco, early thirteenth century. August: a peasant flailing wheat. The coif on his head and the *braies* with side slits are both made of white linen.

waterproof in the Middle Ages. Waxed cloth was used mainly for making window blinds but in fourteenth-century England its use for outer garments is also recorded.

Cotton fabrics imported from Egypt and the Middle East were known in Europe before the thirteenth century, when pure cotton or cotton mixed with hemp or with linen began to be woven in northern Italy and Spain, and later in southern Germany. These 'fustians' have the same twill suface as serge; they are strong and were relatively expensive, often used for making doublets and for making summer outer garments and winter underwear. Unspun cotton was used as wadding between two thicknesses of cloth, as a lining for the doublets and other padded garments that were fashionable from the thirteenth to the fifteenth century.

ANIMAL SKINS

Concurrently a fashion developed that brought about a frantic demand for fur in the princely courts and did away temporarily with the suspicion surrounding animal skins – for centuries a symbol of belonging to the uncivilised world. Fur was now civilised, having been tamed by its cost and by the way it was used, externally or hidden from view. Apart from the occasional fur coat, lined with another fur, worn by court dandies at the end of the fourteenth century and obviously a revival of the style of coat worn in the high Middle Ages, furs were used to line woollen garments. A glimpse could be caught of them in the vent of a coat when its wearer moved, or they would be hidden under the fabric of closed garments, discreetly visible only at the edges, at the hem, neck or wrists.

Western Europe at this time still had a dense covering of woodland and lakes, and animal life abounded. There was also an active fur trade with countries around the North Sea and the Baltic, with skins coming from northern and eastern Europe: beaver and fox, but especially squirrel (miniver), marten and the sumptuous sable. Many different furs were used, depending on what was currently the fashion: the early strong predilection for white or grey gave way after the end of the fourteenth century to a marked preference for dark colours, particularly for men's clothing. Princely account books give a glimpse of the quantity as well as the diversity of furs ued in court costume. Almost any item of clothing, from boots to hats, can be fur-lined, including the suits of matching gown and mantle cut from the same material and accessories such as gloves or mittens and broad-brimmed beaver hats. Use of the most highly prized furs – ermine, vair and sable – was restricted by price as well as by legislation to a narrow category of wearers. Although by the end of the fourteenth century the richest members of the bourgeoisie were sometimes dressed in vair, the demand for fur remained much higher in court circles, both in qualitative and quantitative terms. Outside the courts fur was worn for practical reasons rather than for ostentation. In the world of merchants and artisans the number of fur-lined gowns decreased with decreasing affluence; the furs employed ranged from fox and wild cat to lamb and rabbit. Among the peasantry a fur-lined wool pelisse was an almost unheard of luxury, but women would frequently own a leather jerkin lined with its own fur; this might be made of lambskin or, more commonly, of rabbit or kid. Men had to make do with simple woollen gowns, plus the occasional leather garment or fur-lined mittens.

The strength of leather and its relative impermeability when thick, plus the softness of the finest skins, made it a material with a wide range of uses. Leather found in archaeological excavations reveals the skill of the leather workers in the preparation of the skins and the many different techniques used in its decoration. Stamped, engraved, cut, embroidered, even sometimes painted, leather was used to make elegant accessories – belts, baldrics, purses, gloves or shoes. Leather was virtually the only material used for making shoes, wood making a brief appearance very late on in the period. From babies' bootees to the thigh boots worn by horsemen, a range of leathers was required.

9 *Psalter.* Meermanno West., The Hague, MS 76 F 13, f.5v, illuminated in Fécamp *c.*1180–1200. May: wearing a mantle lined with spotted ermine over his shoulders, a knight sets out for the hunt with his falcon perched on his gauntlet.

The commonest type of shoe, according to archaeological sources, was a boot laced with leather, pointed or not according to the period. Later a strip of leather fastened with a metal buckle was worn round the ankle.

The protective quality of leather gave it a large number of uses. It was made into outer garments for tradesmen and artisans; while leggings of chamois leather are documented as being worn by princes on horseback, many other horsemen must have worn similar garments. Leather was used to protect particular parts of the body in a variety of professional activities: aprons and gloves, gloves for falconry and so on.

METAL

According to surviving documents, princes and the aristocracy wore quilted garments under their armour; perhaps the leather doublets found at archaeological sites and belonging to the less exalted classes were similarly used to protect the body from contact with suits of armour.

The coat of ring mail was a leather garment reinforced with metal plates, but the more expensive types of armour, as techniques improved, did not need the leather support. The armour of the common soldiery, on the other hand, was of lesser quality and sometimes consisted only of 'boiled' leather. Leather continued to play an important role, even when suits of armour were entirely made of metal; the pieces of metal were held together by leather thongs and straps and were also often lined with leather as well.

The increasing skill of metalworkers, notably their gradual mastery of how to combine metals, is evident in the development of the armour worn by the ruling classes. Neither armour of metal plates fixed on leather nor coats of mail made of rings of wire-drawn iron were medieval inventions. The idea of breast plates was taken by the Roman army from the Gauls and other invaders. The techniques of wire-drawing and iron-plate hammering were gradually being perfected. Steelmaking helped to improve the resistance of metal while the quality of arrows and power of crossbows made better protection a necessity. The use of steel strips for brigandines and the combination of strips and rings for jazerants demonstrate the spread of high-level metalworking skills throughout the Western world; nevertheless, the possession of a complete suit of armour, made to measure and costing large sums of money, remained the privilege of a very few. Such centres of production as Milan and later Nuremberg became internationally renowned.

Non-ferrous and precious metals were of only subsidiary importance in armour, as also in civilian clothing. Their decorative role gave them prominence, however, even when their function was unassuming. Even shoe buckles and belt clasps, made of alloys of copper or tin, bore elaborate ornamentation in imitation of the brilliance and refinement of the goldsmith's handiwork.

Wood appeared only towards the end of the period and was used for the thick soles of pattens or galoshes, worn over light shoes and held in place by leather thongs. Wood was sometimes replaced by cork, but this type of footwear was not very widespread. Clogs hollowed out from solid blocks of wood were not made until the sixteenth century. Various ligneous materials, for example lime-tree bark and split hazel or willow switches, were used (as was straw) for making hats in the Middle Ages. The wide-brimmed hats worn by peasants have been made familiar by pictures illustrating haymaking or harvesting. Late medieval documents attest to the fact that, lined with cloth or even silk, they were also worn by members of the upper classes.

CHAPTER THREE

The Acquisition of Clothing

INFORMATION ON THE MEANS BY WHICH medieval families acquired clothing is very patchy, though it is certain that a great deal depended on social class. It is possible to discover where and by what means a fourteenth- or fifteenth-century prince bought his textiles, furs, linings and accessories, and who stitched and embroidered them, and also to have some idea of what happened to the clothes once they were in use; information concerning members of the middle classes is much scarcer, and of the lower classes almost non-existent.

DOMESTIC ACTIVITIES

Making clothes at home played an important role, and methods of doing so varied. The making of textiles, particularly spinning, is abundantly illustrated by artists and the omnipresence of such activities is confirmed by such archaeological finds as spindles, carding combs and, in damp ground, bobbins and distaffs. Well-documented by archaeologists at the height of the Middle Ages, weaving at home gradually died out as the urban craft industry developed. Dressmaking at home is revealed in excavations by finds of thimbles and sewing scissors. Images of the Virgin and saints sewing or knitting, while less numerous than representations of women spinning, are undoubtedly inspired by everyday reality. The setting is generally urban and the Virgin is shown weaving ribbons or girdles or doing embroidery. This kind of work, first recorded in the women's quarters of the great royal or imperial houses, then became an occupation enjoyed by noblewomen and their daughters before spreading to the upper classes in the towns; inventories of the belongings of townswomen refer to embroidery frames and looms for fringe-making. In the iconography of the period Eve is shown spinning like any humble shepherdess or peasant woman. Spinning with a distaff, later with a wheel, was one of the only money-making activities women could engage in at home. The thread spun at home was not intended solely for family use; selling thread in the skein, or spinning to order were both common practices. Although the development of urban crafts focussed primarily on men for processing activities, cloth weaving was often the responsibility of women; thread spun at home remained the property of whoever brought it to the weaver. The small number of undergarment makers cited among urban manual workers implies that linen undergarments were usually made at home. Some of the princely ledgers make it clear that this work was carried out by chambermaids or by women hired on a daily basis. Like the other fabrics used in the confection of the royal wardrobe, the linens stitched by these women were not made at home.

Making Clothes to Measure

Clothing for a prince and his retinue would naturally be made to order, from good quality new materials bought for the purpose. Fabrics might be bought by the bale and kept in stock, particularly the most expensive ones: the English royal family established a warehouse in the heart of the City of London, the Royal Wardrobe, to hold their stocks of fabric. In capital cities fabrics would be purchased from the agents of large companies, often Italian; or a representative of the purchaser would be sent to larger centres of production or commerce to choose stuffs and valuable furs of a quality seldom found in shops. Less exclusive fabrics like the woollen cloth used for everyday wear or for servants' clothing, linen or items of haberdashery, would be purchased from merchants in the local town. On the other hand, when the manufacture of armour became very specialised the habit grew up of ordering it directly from the best-known centres: a messenger bearing the prince's exact measurements on a paper pattern would be ordered to return with the required harness or brigandine. The retinue of craftsmen attached to each court would include an armourer, selected from the most skilled practitioners of the craft; his job would be to adjust, repair and maintain the pieces of armour and coats of mail.

Tailors, furriers and embroiderers played a more obvious role in the prince's final appearance. The sums they were paid for their work seem derisory in comparison with the value of the materials they were working with; the title of 'valet', however, made sure that they were not mistaken for mere servants. They were comfortably lodged in town in houses often rented for them by the prince. The generosity of the prince made it possible for the most cherished of these crafts-men to adopt an almost aristocratic lifestyle, very different from the lifestyle of the local artisans as they toiled away for a much less exalted clientèle. It is not possible to estimate their role in the progress of fashion but, as they were close to the prince and in charge of his wardrobe, they were admirably well placed to keep a watchful eye on the sources of new inspiration – the foreign fashions glimpsed while travelling, or brought to the court by ambassadors from abroad, and the daring innovations sported by the younger members of the chivalrous class, who hoped to attract the attention of the sovereign or some rich heiress.

Royal tailors and seamstresses were not always sufficiently skilled for the tasks they faced; contemporary trade regulations record excep-tions made to the ordinary regulations for any piece of work carried out for the king. The prince's tailor or furrier exercised his art for a strictly limited number of people. Each adult member of the ruling family would have his own staff, and most of those in receipt of fab-rics from outside would have their clothes made away from home, if they were not highly enough placed to have their own private tailor.

Even if tradesmen were less specialised than their counterparts in the largest cities, every town offered a bewildering choice of shops – drapers, dressmakers, cobblers, hosiers as well as hatmakers, embroi-derers and haberdashers: everyone, from townsman to courtier, could shop for what he needed and order the clothing he required. Although the regulations laid down by the city authorities were aimed partly at quality control, they were also concerned with the qualifications of those joining the profession, the annual and daily working hours, and the apportionment of prerogatives between 'trades' that were becoming both more numerous and more spe-cialised. Working conditions and actual working practices can be glimpsed in the few surviving images and also in account books and inventories, although these tend to belong to the later period. For the common people, orders were placed and clothes tried on in the shop, which was furnished in the simplest manner; the clothes that were finished and awaiting collection, and those being made and awaiting the finishing touches, would hang on a wooden pole. The master tai-lor would cut out clothes at a large wooden table on which his assis-tants, whose job it was to assemble and stitch the clothes, sat

10 and 11   *Livre du Roi Florimont*. Bibliothèque Nationale, Paris, Fr. 12566,
f.139 and f.92v, 1418. A tailor and his assistant calling at a private house; the assistant is carrying a measuring rod and shears, and a bolt of cloth on his head.
Clothes were fitted on a tailor's dummy as well as on the client himself.

cross-legged. Their only tools were a few pairs of scissors, large and
small, thimbles and needles. Grander folk would receive their tailor
and his assistants at home.

The town tailor would make gowns and overgarments, chaperons
and *houppelandes*, from fabrics bought by his clients from the draper's
shop. He would provide only the thread, as payments made 'for

thread and stitching' make clear; silken thread would be used for expensive fabrics, linen or hemp for everyday clothes. He was not only employed making new clothes: his order would include repairs and making over, the reversing of a worn or faded gown, the turning or patching of a collar. Studies of the finds from archaeological excavations in London, on the banks of the Thames provide precise information on the cutting and stitching techniques in use for fairly humble clothing: they confirm that clothes were cut in a number of quite sophisticated ways, but that the stitches used to sew the pieces together and for hemming were of the simplest.

Some producers of clothing provided their own raw materials and this must have improved their profit margins very considerably. The importance of the specialised trades (apart from tailoring) fluctuated according to the importance of the items they produced in the fashions of the day. Trade for doublet makers, for example, increased to keep abreast of the fashion for quilted garments consisting of several layers of cloth wadded with cotton. Hosiers grew prosperous as masculine dress shortened and narrowed, showing off the leg to advantage; they would have ready-made hose in the shop but better quality fabrics awaited the wealthier, more demanding clients, who insisted on made-to-measure hose. Some hosiers became considerable cloth merchants as well. The furrier, too, sold ready-made clothes and linings for everyday wear: capes for peasants or warm linings for woollen gowns. Good quality skins were sold individually and were used for the visible parts of the linings, the collars and cuffs. The attachment of fur linings to woollen clothes seems to have been one of the tailor's jobs: at any rate lined gowns occur in the lists of work in progress or completed in some of the contemporary inventories.

The work of the shoemaker, less prestigious than that of the furrier, seems also to have involved a large proportion of ready-to-wear items. Close inspection of the archaeological evidence suggests that the sole stitched on to a welt offered considerable advantages, particularly in damp conditions. The most commonly found shapes (the ankle-length boot was the most popular) and their fastenings remained simple. The London excavations have produced a number of examples of fine sandals, similar to the sandals worn by royalty in contemporary paintings, and also thick-soled pattens, in favour with elegant townsfolk in the fourteenth and fifteenth centuries; the techniques used to produce and decorate expensive footwear – fancy cutwork, engraving, stamping and even sometimes painting – can be studied in detail.

The great diversity of headdresses, combined with changing fashions, used the skills of several different trades. Only *chaperons* of woollen cloth were made by tailors. Furriers provided linings, or made hats entirely of fur. More ephemeral hats made from flowers or peacock feathers were soon supplanted by the fashion for crown-shaped hats. Gold and precious stones were copied in base metals, glass and gilded ribbons. The vogue for gold ribbons, braid and gold-smiths' work brought prosperity for a time to makers of hats and headdresses in the thirteenth and fourteenth centuries. At the same period the development of felt-making produced a reasonably priced material for masculine headgear.

READY-MADE CLOTHING

Felt caps and hats came to be sold not only by the people who made them but at the mercers' shops that were springing up everywhere, like medieval department stores. Among the innumerable other items of clothing that could be bought there were coifs and cotton or silk veils for women, straw hats and nightcaps for men, knitted caps, protective stuffed *bourrelets*, knitted socks and hose for children, and gloves and fur-lined mittens for all. To help make clothes fit, haberdashers also offered buttons, thongs, long laces and a large selection of belts. The most sumptuous belts would have buckles, pendants and appliquéd plates of precious metal and gold, and would be made to order by goldsmiths; trade laws in the late Middle Ages attempted in vain to prohibit haberdashers from selling accessories made of gold plate. At that time their shops stocked large quantities of straps and belts, and less frequently, demi-belts decorated with brass, iron or tin. Items for women to hang on their belts included purses, made of cloth or soft leather, and needlecases, while men were offered larger purses and knives in sheaths. Some haberdashers sold clerical garb, linen albs and rough woollen or fustian chasubles, while others had a whole section devoted to armour.

The mercery trade was run by successful businessmen in the towns and penetrated deep into the countryside thanks to the markets held in every village; pedlars took it even farther afield. This coverage gainsays the traditional view, based on contemporary trading regulations, of the way supply met demand in the Middle Ages. In the mercer's store the client was no longer in direct contact with the manufacturer marketing his own product. The circulation of finished products, many of them mass-produced and of very little value, marks the progressive separation of production from sales. This explains the diffusion through the entire social hierarchy of large numbers of accessories and small items of personal adornment found by archaeologists in excavations in villages as well as in towns.

Paradoxically, there is more information about the ornamentation of costume and the way peasants and modest townsfolk came by their finery than about the way in which costumes were made. Low-priced dress fabrics figure among the stocks of certain drapers, but there is no record of any tailors living in villages. Perhaps dressmaking was exclusively a female profession and therefore deemed unworthy of mention. Alternatively, relatively simple garments, exempt from the vagaries of fashion, may have all been made at home.

GIFTS AND HAND-OUTS: NEW AND OLD

Throughout the medieval period a significant proportion of the clothing supply escaped commercial channels. At all levels of society gifts between equals, or to inferiors, kept fabrics and items of clothing in circulation. In the Carolingian and early medieval period kings would receive presents of sumptuous silks from ambassadors from the Orient, and the best of Western woollen cloth would be given to them in exchange. As late as the fifteenth century textiles and richly decorated pieces of weaponry were exchanged between Christian and Muslim princes, from one side of the Mediterranean to the other. Under the feudal system certain gifts were connected with rites of passage. The suzerain would present scarlet mantles to the young warriors whom he dubbed knights; a lady would give a wedding trousseau to her serving maid. Princely ledgers of the late Middle Ages reveal other, more diverse liberalities: clothing of royal grandeur made by the king's tailor for the holder of some important office, whether a courtier or a visitor; lengths of cloth, accessories or headgear distributed to local women.

Although distributions of cloth were sometimes transformed into gifts of money, service by noblemen or commoners to a prince, lord or municipal authorities was rewarded once or twice a year by a gift or 'livery'. The custom of wearing black as a sign of mourning and of imposing it on an entire court was introduced fairly late, but, like the

liveries, it involved virtually everyone figuring in the prince's household accounts. In fact, these gifts of cloth fall into the same network
of obligation towards employees as the artisan's agreement to clothe
and shoe his apprentice, or the peasant's promise on taking over his
aged parents' land to provide them with food and a new camelin
gown each year. On the other hand, when a king distributed his worn
gowns to his valets, or his ceremonial dress and horses' harness to the
equerries who served him at a tournament, this was once again part
of the system of the distribution of gifts, in money or in kind, to
members of the household in conformity with the ideal of largesse
cultivated by the chivalrous class.

In the hierarchy of gifts, medieval faith placed those made to God,
or to his representatives on earth – churches, abbeys, convents – at
the top. The mighty would make gifts to the cathedrals or churches
they attended, or to the pilgrimage chapels they visited; these gifts
consisted of liturgical vestments and ornaments of an opulence that
reflected the rank of the donor. In accordance with the teachings of
the Gospels, in which Christ represents the poor among men,
Christians are obliged to perform works of charity, one of which consists of clothing the naked. Many accounts of the manner in which
this duty was accomplished survive, in the lives of saints as well as in
secular literature. From the time when account ledgers became com-
monplace in princely households in the fourteenth century, these
daily acts of charity were supervised by the chaplain and distributions
of clothing were entered only in exceptional circumstances. During
Easter ceremonies, on Maundy Thursday, the poor represented the
Apostles and received the gift of a new suit. They can be seen in representations of princely funerals at even the most modest of courts:
thirteen mourners wearing the same material as the courtiers.

The custom of writing a will developed earlier than the habit of
keeping accounts, and the study of wills reveals more about bequests
in general than about gifts of clothing in particular. Some gifts of
clothing come into the category of charitable bequests. Lords and
members of the middle classes might order that certain paupers
invited to the funeral service and repast should be given new clothing for the occasion. Other well-to-do folk would concentrate their
generosity on monasteries of the mendicant orders, even specifying
the type of cloth that was to be purchased with their money. The
church chosen by the testator for his obsequies would also often
be rewarded with gifts of textiles for carefully itemised purposes. A

12   *Statuts du collège de Jean Hubant.* Archives Nationales, Paris, A E/ɪɪ 408, f.7, illuminated in Paris in 1346. College students handing out shoes and clothing to the poor.

valuable coloured fabric would be used first as a pall on the coffin, and would then be transformed into a chasuble and donated to the church. Later, when black was adopted as the colour for all funeral hangings, it remained the custom for the testator to bequeath a chasuble to the church in which he was interred. Among the less wealthy, bequests were far more modest, consisting sometimes of used clothing left to charitable institutions, particularly to hospices for the poor. Some of the probate inventories justify the absence of clothing belonging to the deceased by stating 'given to God', thereby linking the law with religious practices.

The motive behind posthumous distributions that were exclusively in favour of family members was quite different. In its broadest sense the family included all those related to the family by blood, or having a spiritual link, and also all those living under the same roof. The best gowns of coloured cloth, lined with fur, and the costliest accessories would be left to the direct descendants and godchildren. In wealthy households, even where the deceased had direct descendants, the domestic servants would not be forgotten, but they would receive only the most ordinary items of clothing. The value of woollen fabrics and of furs, always high and sometimes significantly so, meant that these bequests played quite a considerable role in the domestic economy of the beneficiaries.

The position occupied in gifts and bequests by bolts of cloth and used clothing demonstrates the lasting value of any item made of

textile fibres, even when second hand. Surviving documents provide
only a glimpse of the second-hand clothing trade, which must have
had wide ramifications. The activities of dealers were monitored by
urban authorities, but the Paris regulations reveal the easy-going
recruitment requirements and the varied nature of the trade. Some
dealers had shops, others walked the streets calling 'gowns and cloaks'
('la robe et la chape') to attract buyers. The nature of the clientèle,
and the many ways in which they came by their merchandise, can
only be surmised. Some beneficiaries of legacies and gifts probably
sold the clothing left to them in the will in order to have money for
other necessities. Rather than pawning an item of clothing with no
hope of redeeming it, others might have been obliged to sell it.
Second-hand clothes dealers could also build up their stocks at public sales held in town market places or in front of the village church.
They would not have been the only bidders, however, and purchasers
of second-hand clothing could avoid the middleman by buying at
public sales.

PART TWO

DEVELOPMENT AND SOCIAL GROUPINGS

CHAPTER FOUR

The History of Working-Class Clothing

RELIABLE ACCOUNTS OF THE WAY ordinary men and women dressed to go about their business are scarce before the thirteenth century. Although towns developed significantly during this century, the vast majority of the population lived in the country in the Middle Ages. Drawings, paintings and sculpture give a picture of these peasants much earlier than do texts. In visual representations, particularly in the carved depictions of the seasons that began to become popular in the twelfth century, it is the shape of the clothing that can best be appreciated. Later, frescoes and illuminated manuscripts on a wide variety of subjects give information about materials, colours and scenery that was often missing from the stylised carvings. Literary texts in general ignore the peasant milieu: when the subject does occur its handling reflects the prejudices, fear and even repulsion felt by the educated ruling classes for the multitude, held in great contempt and indeed regarded by many as hardly human. In some areas, in the thirteenth century and even more so in the fourteenth and fifteenth, documents such as wills, inventories and deeds have survived, and these help to give a clearer picture of the working man's wardrobe. The information contained in these documents reveals the type of clothing worn and the outfits possessed even by the poorest members of society.

From the Carolingian period until the fourteenth century clothing developed extraordinarily slowly, in some cases hardly changing at all. The long, full robe worn by the Romanized élite remained a privilege of this social group. The humility of even the highest ranks of 'barbarians' is well known. Charlemagne's chroniclers record the fact that he remained loyal to Frankish dress, which was in fact very similar to the daily wear of most of the inhabitants of the Empire. Most of the clothing worn by country folk and lower-class townsfolk in medieval Europe can be traced back to these two sources.

The Elements of Costume

The main garment worn over the centuries, although its name may have varied, has always been a kind of tunic with sleeves, calf-length for women, sometimes above the knee for men. The *saie* or short cape worn by the Franks adorned the shoulders of labourers as well as warriors, as can be seen in the ninth-century *Stuttgart Psalter*. Carvings of the four seasons later show peasants in winter wearing short capes with hoods, or sometimes coats with sleeves that are directly descended from the Gallo-Roman *bardocucullus*.

Peasant women are less frequently portrayed but appear to have worn (until the fourteenth century) a veil, full or not so full, over their tunics and covering their head and shoulders. Coats appear to have been restricted to the wealthier classes. The iconography gives little idea of what was worn under the gown. Late medieval texts mention gowns and 'cottes', probably more crudely made, worn under the gown. The names given to certain items of feminine attire after the thirteenth century are often archaic and suggest that popular costume altered hardly at all over the years. The only warm garment, mentioned several times, in the posthumous inventories of Burgundian women in the fourteenth century, the fur pelisse, poses a problem. The explanation for its absence from any representation may be that it was worn under the gown or cotte. The only references to this item of clothing concern its material, a cheap fur – either baby goat or lamb, rabbit or cat, and its border of braid bought from the mercer's shop. This information suggests that the garment in question was a waistcoat of animal skin with the fur inside and under the gown.

Was body linen worn under woollen tunics only after the fourteenth century? This contention has been sustained by historians for more than a century but has never been properly justified. The scarcity of documents plus the fact that the overgarments completely hid any undergarments until the fourteenth century have probably encouraged this interpretation. Images of the seasons representing peasants only partly clothed taking part in summer activities attest to the wearing of shifts, *braies* (loose trousers) and cloth headdresses by the labouring classes. Fuller information, available for the late medieval period, makes it clear that undergarments were few but were worn by all and sundry.

The shift consisted of a full tunic with sleeves, long for women,

13 *Stuttgart Psalter.* Württembergische Landesbibliothek, Stuttgart, fol. 23, f.124v, illuminated in northern France (probably at Saint-Germain-des-Prés), *c.* 820–830. A peasant, in Carolingian times, labouring in the fields wearing a short tunic and a small flowing cape or *saie* of the type inherited from the Franks; his hose are held up by cross-garters. Apart from the garters this style of dress hardly changed for the next five hundred years.

shorter for men, usually made of hemp; linen, which was much more expensive, was restricted to a small élite. *Braies* were either long and full or short and tight-fitting; they had been worn by the inhabitants of Gaul and by all the 'barbarian' peoples, having been inherited from the horsemen of the steppes of Central Asia, and were worn exclusively by men. They were in everyday use right up to the very end of the Middle Ages and were always made of toile, i.e., linen or hemp.

Body linen should also include caps and bonnets. Close-fitting linen bonnets, tied under the chin and called 'coifs', were widely worn by men in the thirteenth century but were gradually abandoned in the fourteenth in favour of large linen kerchiefs. These were wrapped around the head as nightcaps by men and were worn as headdresses, day and night, by women. Although it is not possible to give a date to each style, masculine headgear, including peasant headgear, was very varied. Caps, wide-brimmed hats and straw hats were worn on their own or with a hood or linen bonnet underneath. The choice for women was more limited, but a linen kerchief or woollen hood could be worn in a variety of ways. The importance of headgear, both male and female, as a sign of personal honour, is demonstrated in many contemporary legal documents: to pull off a woman's headdress or to knock a man's hat off was a serious offence that incurred severe punishment.

Legwear and shoes were not in constant use by the working classes – contemporary iconography shows many bare feet. The remarkable

14   *Psautier à l'usage de la chartreuse de Montrieux*. Bibliothèque
Nationale, Paris, Lat. 1073 A, f.4, fourteenth century. The angel
appears to the shepherds, who, like other peasants, had to be out
in all weathers and wore a variety of headgear to protect themselves: hoods, coifs, hooded capes and wide-brimmed hats.

smooth floors of beaten earth uncovered by archaeologists in
labourer's cottages would seem to confirm this. Images and written
texts, however, suggest that by the late Middle Ages 'hose' were

generally worn. It is not easy to ascertain from illustrations (which for many years were the only source of information) at what period these fabric stockings became popular; it is difficult to distinguish them from *braies* tied up with cloth strips, which had been in use since Carolingian times.

The peasants and lower classes are generally depicted wearing shoes. Both iconography and archaeology show the most usual footwear to have been a sort of lace-up boot reaching ankle-height; after the fourteenth century the boot was closed by a small buckle on a leather flap. Late medieval illustrations are more detailed and show peasants in wooden-soled shoes. There is no archaeological evidence of any metal studding under the shoes, nor of clogs cut from a single piece of wood.

Inventories of the belongings of peasants, paupers and female servants, found in archives in Italy, France and Switzerland, give a clear picture of the contents of the wardrobe of members of the working classes. Underwear appears in short supply; items of underwear were often omitted from the lists anyway because they would be donated to charitable institutions to be distributed to the poor after the death of their owner. In many instances only one main garment, the gown or *cotta*, is mentioned, to which may be added a hooded mantle for men and a pelisse with a bonnet for women. One or two linen squares to cover the head (*couvre-chef*), occasionally a felt or straw hat and a pair each of hose and shoes complete the strictly functional wardrobe. The few items of clothing would be worn until they were completely worn out. The descriptions supplied by the people drawing up the inventories ('old', 'worn', 'holey', 'patched', 'turned') vividly convey the poor state of the clothing and, in a more general way, the mediocre quality of the more miserable items.

The same documents give valuable information about the materials from which the clothing was made. By this time fabrics were not made at home. The artisans who wove the hemp and linen spun at home remained closely involved at a domestic level. The production of woollen cloth had developed in the towns to a scale that was often almost industrial; in the fourteenth and fifteenth centuries it began to shift outwards into the surrounding villages. In spite of the technical progress that was made, most peasants and poor townsfolk had access only to products of mediocre quality. The few pieces of underwear they owned were of hemp or other coarse cloth which became whiter and softer only after repeated washings. Outer garments were made from the cheapest fabrics in the draper's range: frieze, beige (undyed wool), rough serge, some of which were undoubtedly woven from wool mixtures. The woollen cloth was almost invariably dyed blue, in all the shades that woad could produce, and the colours would fade as the years passed. Anyone possessing more brightly coloured gowns – reds, greens, purples – belonged to a higher social class, at least in the fourteenth century. The overall impression would have been drab. For men the main garment, the gown, *cotta* or cloak, would usually be made of coarse-looking cloth, undyed, therefore brownish or greyish; the blue of the hood would sometimes add a touch of colour. At the equivalent social level the women would look a bit more elegant in blue woollen gowns or *cotte*, often with a red hood.

Determining the number of items of clothing owned by an individual is no simple matter. Before a posthumous inventory was drawn up, some of the garments may have been removed by the heirs or given away as charity; others, like shoes and to a lesser extent hats and linen, were often omitted because they were of no particular value. Unlike Tuscan peasants or city dwellers (even poor ones) most Burgundian villagers in the fourteenth century possessed no change of gown. For them, to dress up meant to put on their best headgear. As circumstances grew easier, however, some items of clothing are described as new and made of coloured cloth; these must have allowed peasants to cut a better figure on high days and holidays.

ADAPTING TO CLIMATIC CONDITIONS

Even though it consisted of so few garments, this wardrobe could, in practice, be combined in different ways as required to protect the body. Climatic conditions and the seasonal cycle obviously varied according to region; generally speaking layers were removed in warm weather and replaced in cold. Italian peasants always wore white, but it is impossible to be sure that their clothing was always made of light fabric, linen or cotton. Inventories drawn up in the countryside around Florence in the fifteenth century do however state that fabrics made of vegetable fibres were used to make outer garments.

Men and women protected themselves against the cold in different ways. Sleeveless capes and coats with sleeves and hoods were worn only by men. Some of the oldest illustrations show fur capes worn with the fur outside. Subsequently such garments became less frequent, possibly because the medieval mind associated animal skins with savagery, but also because technical progress had improved the output of the textile industry. Cloth made from wool that still retained some of its natural oils provided protection against damp. This resistance could be increased by fulling, a process of felting woollen fabric to make it almost completely waterproof. The invention of the fulling mill reduced the cost of this procedure and made such fabrics more widely accessible. Archaeological samples confirm that fulling was now used on cloth of varying quality, and not just on fine wool. Another process that was even more effective for making fabric waterproof was waxing, certainly used in England in the late Middle Ages but not very widespread, probably on account of the high cost of wax. According to surviving documents, outer garments of leather were not much in use, although they were less expensive. This impression may in fact need revising, especially with regard to areas of central and eastern Europe such as Poland, where archaeological sites have often yielded considerable quantities of fragments of leather clothing. Finally, if the author of a treatise written in 1379 is to be believed, it is an overgarment of thick canvas that 'protects the shepherd from the rain': the 'surplice', the same shape as the *cotta*, was a kind of smock (at that period the term was not reserved for the garment worn by priests). The wide-brimmed felt hat also provided effective protection from rain.

Women were less exposed to the vagaries of the weather than men because they were less involved in agricultural labour away from home; their warm clothing did not amount to much. For gowns they preferred fine wool to the men's coarse frieze; the pelisse or sleeveless jacket must have helped to compensate for the difference in weight. In colder regions like Scandinavia or Poland the abundance of wild animals and the severity of the climate probably meant that fur would have been worn more regularly; documentation relating to working-class life is unfortunately very scarce and refers to a later period. Some of the surviving illustrations suggest another method whereby women may have protected themselves from a shower: the length and fullness of their gowns may have allowed them to pull part of the train over their head.

The Birth of Working Clothes

In studying labourers' clothing, it is always difficult to distinguish between garments designed for protection against the weather and those adapted for particular tasks, for example, harvesting or haymaking, both of which constituted heavy labour. The images reflect the ideology of the dominant oligarchy and nearly always depict the working population pursuing the activity for which their social position befitted them: namely, work. Although it was not until the nineteenth century that professional clothing with complex specifications was developed, medieval iconography and, later, texts illustrate the early appearance of working clothes tailored for specific tasks. Clothes could be made to suit requirements in other ways too, by being worn in a particular way (the most frequent) or by the addition or modification of an item of clothing to suit a particular activity.

Having as small a number of clothes at his disposal as he did, the artisan used his ingenuity in adapting them to the movements accompanying his daily work. If, for instance, the sleeves of his tunic got in his way he would roll them up or wear a sleeveless tunic. Haymakers and harvesters need complete freedom of movement of the arms; fishermen and plasterers need to avoid getting their clothes wet. Potters working with wet clay prefer to work with bare arms, as do butchers, fishmongers and bakers, all of whom work with potentially dirty foodstuffs,.

Freedom of leg movement is also indispensable for many activities. Even before the thirteenth century peasants are depicted wearing tunics with a slit on either side, which allowed a piece of clothing that was in the way to be hitched up, either in front or to one side. Peasant women also wore tunics with slits at the side, over a long linen smock. In the absence of side slits the overgarment would simply be lifted up and tucked into the belt. The individual panels of a gown or apron could serve a useful purpose as well: hitched over one arm they made a large pocket in which fruit could be carried when picked.

This method of adapting everyday dress to different circumstances was mainly individual and *ad hoc*. Occasionally, however, a transformation would catch on and be generally adopted, as was the case with the major agricultural tasks of the summer, performed in great heat and requiring strength and agility. The requirements of the climate and the need to use specific tools meant that these activities were accomplished wearing the minimum of clothing. The thresher is

15 *Maciejowski Bible*. Pierpont Morgan Library, New York, MS 638, f.12v, illuminated in Paris *c*.1250–55. Labourers flailing wheat: one of them wears his linen *braies* tucked up and attached to his waistband with small cords; another has pulled the front panels of his gown up and tied them at the sides.

shown working stripped to the waist, wearing only his *braies*. Although *braies* with a side vent would have allowed greater freedom of movement they are not often portrayed. Some illustrations show *braies* worn pulled up and tied round the waist with the cords which were usually worn round the calves.

Labourers wearing loose shifts are frequently depicted. This linen garment was usually worn to mid-thigh length, belted or loose, over short *braies* that it covered completely. The shift was the garment always worn for haymaking, and also sometimes for harvesting and for treading grapes. The same garment was worn on building sites by labourers responsible for turning the capstan, a task that demanded sustained effort and caused the labourer to perspire heavily. Charcoal burners, potters and bakers all worked near sources of heat and many worked wearing a loose linen shift and nothing else.

16   Pietro de Crescenzi: *Livre des profits champêtres*. Musée
Condé, Chantilly, MS 340 (603), f.207, illuminated by
Colin d'Amiens (known as the Master of the Geneva
Boccaccio) in western France *c*.1460–75. These reapers are
wearing wide-brimmed hats to protect them from the sun,
and knee-length white linen shirts with side slits and deep V-
necks.

Certain accessories played an important role in the adaptation of
normal clothing to professional requirements. In the absence of pock-
ets the belt would be used for hanging tools and other useful items.
Besides a multi-purpose knife, keys and a purse, a peasant would hang
a small container for his whetstone from his belt, and a shepherd a
small box of ointment for his animals. A labourer would slip the
handle of his trowel or pruning knife into his belt when he needed to
use two hands.

Haymakers and harvesters wore straw hats to protect themselves
from extremes of sunshine, and other headdresses were adopted in
relation to specific activities. For dirty tasks like treading grapes, or for
the preparation of clay and throwing of pots in the pottery, the hair
would be covered by a coif or bonnet. Kerchiefs were worn in professions relating to foodstuffs and requiring a certain degree of
hygiene – bakery and butchery. Blacksmiths, potters, glassmakers and

17   Misericord. Cathedral of Saint John the Baptist, Saint-Jean-de-Maurienne, 1498. Three-fingered working gloves made of fur-lined leather.

others whose trade was dependent on fire would cover their heads to protect their hair from sparks. Representations are not quite numerous enough to indicate whether variations in the shape of headgear are exclusively related to chronology. Most headgear was made of linen: the close-fitting bonnet that covered the ears, the bonnet worn on the back of the head or the square of fabric tied over the hair.

Images of gloves used for work are few and generally of late date. One of the most distinct comes from the stalls in the church of Saint-Jean-de-Maurienne and dates from the fifteenth century. The quality of the sculpture makes it possible to observe that the gloves are made of lambskin with the skin outside and the fur inside. The gloves have three 'fingers', which would have given the wearer relative freedom of movement. Peasants labouring, cutting wood and even haymaking are depicted wearing gloves of this type. Furniture inventories and builders' account books confirm that sheepskin gloves were worn by masons and by other workers using dangerous tools or corrosive materials. In the case of shepherds and fishermen, whose activity took place mainly in winter and during Lent, gloves were worn for warmth as well as for protection.

Strictly speaking, the only item of working clothing in widespread use throughout the Middle Ages was the apron. Its function was largely dependent on the sex and activity of the wearer. Foodsellers, like fishmongers and bakers, would wear an apron when behind the counter to protect their gowns. Peasant women wore aprons almost all the time, at least from the period when illustrations abound; the length of the aprons varied, but most women seem to have worn them ankle-length, sometimes full-length and completely covering the skirt. Written texts endorse what is suggested by study of the pictures: women's aprons were always of undyed linen, white or occasionally reddish. Not until the final years of the fifteenth century and the early sixteenth did coloured aprons begin to appear, with preference given to bright red and bright blue. The medieval apron was tied round the waist and had no bib; it was neither gathered nor pleated and was fastened by ties of the same fabric, or, occasionally, a piece of coloured braid.

A peasant woman would wear her apron for all domestic activities, both indoors (particularly for cooking) and out. She would keep it on for going to fetch water, watching the herds, milking cows and sheep and also for working in the fields – grape picking in the season, or tying sheaves of corn at harvest time. In the fifteenth century the apron became an integral part of the peasant woman's gown. She would wear it when she took food to farm labourers or harvesters in the fields. Its connection with work gradually began to disappear as it began to be worn during festivities as well, symbolised in contemporary iconography by the dance of the shepherds.

For men the apron was restricted to specific activities, and was worn only for dirty tasks such as filling barrels, or for slaughtering and butchering pigs or cows: a white apron knotted to the belt offered protection against splashes of blood. Men's aprons were generally shorter than women's and seem to have been made from rough linen, invariably white. Often they consisted simply of a rectangle of cloth without ties; the corners would be knotted behind.

Although not widely used by men in the rural environment, aprons were customarily worn by certain artisans. Blacksmiths are always represented wearing an apron, which could be knotted behind or (for those with a bib) either clipped or pinned to the undergarment on the chest or held up by braces. For all metalworkers leather (often tanned hides) was frequently worn instead of heavy linen: aprons are mentioned in Burgundian inventories in the possession of blacksmiths, knife-makers and tinsmiths, all of whom had to protect themselves and their clothing from sparks and fragments of molten metal. A thick, solid apron also protected the farrier from contact with horses' hoofs. Sometimes the tanned leather would retain the shape of the animal it was made from, or it might have broad straps below. Usually, however, it would be trimmed to a rectangular shape like the fabric aprons.

The shape and materials of the aprons worn by woodworkers (carpenters or coopers, for example) were just as varied, as were those worn by stonemasons to protect themselves from fragments of stone

18 *King Wenceslas Bible.* Österreichische Nationalbibliothek, Vienna, MS 2760, f.146, illuminated in Bohemia
*c.*1389–1400. A blacksmith hammering metal: a long leather
apron protects him from sparks.

and splashes of mortar. Painters and their assistants who mixed the
colours had the same need for protection. The most frequently portrayed members of the food trade, bakers and butchers, always wore
linen aprons. The apron was not solely used by tradespeople for protection against external aggression or stain. The goldsmith is shown at
his bench with a tanned leather apron which he uses to collect scraps
of precious metal that have fallen on the floor while he has been
engraving or polishing.

It was an exception rather than the rule that an ordinary piece of
attire would be worn repeatedly for a given activity until it eventually became identified as the professional wear for that activity. This
occurred with the sowing apron, which was derived from a traditional item of clothing. For centuries peasants used wooden seed
holders, or a bucket, but at the same time would carry the seeds in a
flap of their outer garment, or in a pocket made by holding the lower
hem of the garment over their arm. In the thirteenth century it
became customary to wear a canvas bag slung across the shoulder, or

19   *Belles Heures de Jean de Berry.* The Cloisters, New York,
f.11, illuminated by Paul and Herman Limbourg *c.*1405–8.
October: the sower is wearing a sowing apron with two
straps fastening behind. Garments of this type appear in
iconographic records from the fourteenth century onwards.

a rectangular piece of cloth knotted over one shoulder or round the
neck and lifted over the arm to form a pocket. The sowing apron
with two shoulder straps tied behind did not become popular until
the fourteenth century; once it had caught on, however, in that particular style, it remained in use almost without modification until the
early twentieth century. The apron was thus specifically tailored to
the needs of the farmer.

Other working garments began gradually to appear in the fourteenth century and particularly in the fifteenth. A flap of cloth at the
back of the hood, covering the shoulders, made carrying heavy or
dirty loads on the back less difficult. During the grape harvest the
hood worn on the head and the flap covering the shoulders and back
prevented the basket of grapes coming into direct contact with the
picker; the same hood, probably made of linen in white or beige, was
used by building workers to carry loads of mortar on their backs. A

20 *Kutna-Hora Gradual.* Österreichische Nationalbibliothek, Vienna, MS 15501, f.1, illuminated in Bohemia *c*.1490. These Bohemian miners are wearing hooded shirts of white linen and leather breeches to protect their legs.

similar garment is worn today by meat porters, but its use in that context is not attested in the Middle Ages. Nor is there any trace in contemporary iconography of some of the working clothes worn over the usual gowns or *cottes* and described in written documents: to work in the fields peasant men and women would put on a 'rochet' or smock made of linen. The same overshirt was also worn by modest townsfolk; the cut must have been very simple, like the cut of the leather smock worn by certain craftsmen.

Even more specialised working clothes were worn for activities requiring special protection. By the end of the Middle Ages bee-keepers were wearing not only masks to cover their heads and upper chests but thick mittens, with the rest of their bodies completely covered by normal clothing. The first appearance of this costume is difficult to date. The eleventh-century manuscripts that make up the devotional *Exultet* contain a number of scenes relating to bees and beekeeping, but the beekeepers are portrayed without any protective clothing and with bare hands. In fourteenth- and fifteenth-century treatises on agriculture, however, the beekeepers are attired in their protective clothing. Another professional activity requiring extra pro-tection was glass blowing; to protect the craftsman from the heat of the furnace a visor that came down below the eyes would be worn, and his hair would be tucked into a turban or hat.

Mining in the Middle Ages was carried out in particularly haz-ardous conditions and entailed great risk. By the late Middle Ages working clothes had evolved that were specially adapted to the pro-fession. In miniatures depicting the silver-mines of Kutna-Hora in Bohemia leather breeches protected the miners from cold and damp and from the rough surface of the rocks; the upper body would be protected by a white shirt and a hood that tied under the chin. Sometimes this outfit would be completed by leather knee pads.

In spite of evidence to the contrary, clothes adapted to particular occupations remained the exception. Most of the activities engaged in by members of the working classes were done in ordinary cloth-ing, occasionally adapted with skill for a particular task. Clothing in general was too expensive for the working populace to choose any-thing but their oldest, most worn-out clothing when they had to per-form rough or dirty tasks.

CHAPTER FIVE

Kings and Warriors: The Ruling Classes and their Fashions

HAVING SWEPT AWAY THE POLITICAL infrastructures of Rome, the Roman peace, barbarian invasions re-established the rule of the warrior caste. By the time that Charlemagne, with the pope's assistance, came to restore the Empire, the social structure of power had been radically altered. Trying to piece together, from the very incomplete ninth-century documents that survive, the manner in which members of the ruling class manifested their political allegiance through their clothing is no easy matter. The narrative texts and illustrated documents of the period, however, although not permitting detailed tracing of the development of the shape of clothes, show clearly how the long tunic and draped toga of the Roman aristocracy were supplanted by the cut and stitched garments of a nation of horsemen. The short Carolingian tunics fitted the figure more closely, allowing freedom of movement and the handling of weapons; they were never longer than knee-length and were worn belted at the waist. The baldric was worn like a scarf over the tunic and held the sword in place. *Braies* or, alternatively, hose, cross-gartered to hold them up, were worn under the tunic. Most of these garments were made of wool, often textured, or of linen. They were decorated with wool or silk braid in contrasting colours, sometimes in complicated geometrical patterns stitched around the neck, the front opening, the wrists and hems. The appearance of a warrior, king or courtier resembled that of a Celt or German before the Roman occupation, or of the peoples who had remained outside the reach of the Roman Empire. Even the big cloak, used as a blanket as well as an item of clothing, seems closer to the tradition of nomadic warriors than it is to the toga worn by high-ranking Romans. At Charlemagne's court the debate about dress was between different 'barbaric' styles: in spite of the Emperor's disapproval, the members of his entourage preferred the shorter *saie* to the long Frankish cloak.

Charlemagne's biographers imply that the members of his

21   *Vie de Saint Aubin d'Angers.* Bibliothèque Nationale, Paris, Nal. 1390, f.2v, illuminated in Angers at the end of the eleventh century. The short tunics have flared, full skirts; the hems, neck-openings and waistbands are decorated with embroidery and braid. The legs are protected by plain-coloured hose.

entourage developed a taste for luxury in dress which was in sharp contrast to the sovereign's moderation. In fact this is a recurrent hagiographer's complaint, made in connection with other 'good' rulers by their chroniclers, themselves generally monks opposed to change and to luxury in personal adornment. Should one therefore disbelieve the description of the emperor going hunting wearing a simple sheepskin over his tunic while his companions wore costumes decorated with peacock and flamingo feathers? In any case, the lesson the emperor wanted to teach when he dragged his finely clad followers through the bushes in pouring rain seems to have been lost on them – the taste for luxury continued unabated.

The warrior class continued to wear the costume of the Carolingian period almost unaltered from the ninth century until the end of the eleventh. Contemporary illustrations and texts show variations in the choice of headdress: hats or ribbons circling the head and the appearance of caps. Tunics flare at the hem and are sometimes cut shorter or slit at the sides, and *braies* are cut with more fullness. These details of dress are unfortunately too scattered for it to be possible to relate any of the practices to a precise ethnic group or geographical location, or to allot them to a particular social class, or even to an exact period. As just noted, chroniclers were ever ready to heap censure on their subjects and take a perverse pleasure in describing extravagant modes of dress which were certainly not common.

WARRIORS AND THE MIRAGE OF THE MEDITERRANEAN WORLD

The expansion of the textile industry is hardly mentioned in Western sources, because all eyes were trained on Byzantium, then enjoying a period of prosperity. The imperial workshops were producing their famous silks, dyed in every shade of purple, often embellished with brocaded patterns in gold or other colours. The word *scharlachen*, used to designate a fabric described as velvet, is first encountered in a text dating from before 1032 and written in Old High German. Although this ancestor of 'scarlet' may not have all the characteristics listed in later trade descriptions, the fabric referred to is without a shadow of doubt fine, plain-coloured, felted and possibly dyed with the most costly dye produced in the West, the 'graine de kermès' from the Mediterranean. All silk at this period was imported from Byzantine or Islamic countries and was accessible only to the emperor, to kings and to a few highly placed dignitaries. 'Scarlet' produced an intense red colour when dyed, red being the colour then considered most prestigious, in the West as elsewhere; in the Middle Ages the medical theory of the humours attributed prophylactic powers to the colour red. Imbued with this potency, scarlet became the emblem of feudal power, and for centuries was the fabric from which the cloak given to young knights at their dubbing ceremony was fashioned.

Both texts and iconography at this period pay more attention to their didactic message than to the day-to-day life of their contemporaries, and it is difficult as a result to establish the scope and duration of the sweeping changes in dress when, at the end of the eleventh century, the long and very full gown was adopted in the northern part of the region. The introduction of this type of garment into north-western Europe (it was already widely worn in the south) is attributed quite plausibly to the knights in the entourage of the Duke of Normandy. Some costume historians suggest that this simply represented a return to the long gowns of Ancient Greece and Rome, whose use persisted in ecclesiastical dress. It would seem more likely that the fashion for long clothes reflected the influence of the clothes worn in areas conquered by the Saracens. In fact, on the periphery of their sphere of influence, the Iberian peninsula, for example, or in Sicily or southern Italy, Christian soldiers had constant if bellicose contact with their Saracen opponents. Their curled hair and full-length ceremonial coats flapping around their legs and arms made their critics judge them to be effeminate and symptomatic of the general slackening of morals. The tunics worn over suits of armour were inspired by this fashion, though with the sleeves narrowed; they were slit in front and behind so that the rider could sit astride the saddle, and sometimes there were side slits as well, dividing the tunic into four panels.

Various aspects of twelfth-century clothing are revealed through the moralists' rantings and ravings, in particular the fashion for pointed shoes. Was the association (which appeared again at a later date) between finery that was pointed in shape and the devil just polemics, or should it be seen as the reaction to provocation by the aristocracy? Making a cult of one's appearance was a feature of the idea of largesse embedded in the code of chivalry, and this was already something of a challenge to the idea of moderation in matters of dress promoted by the religious orders. Shoes with points curving upwards had appeared spasmodically throughout the preceding centuries, but it was during the twelfth century that shoes with points that curled horizontally like rams' horns and little tongues that hung above the heel were introduced.

MEDIEVAL CLASSICISM

Another survival from the uncivilised world, the fur used to line and edge garments, was now bidden to a more glamorous future; it was no longer used solely for utilitarian purposes, as it had been in former centuries. Garments were now trimmed with fur as a sign of wealth and power. Images of Saint Martin, the soldier who halved his cloak with a stroke of his sword to give half to a beggar, show that the knight's cloak was embellished with a lining of light-coloured fur. The most sought-after furs were in fact white ermine with its black spots, pale grey vair and the grey and white of miniver (menu-vair), consisting of the grey back and white stomach of this small member of the squirrel family. The armorial system, which was developing at this period, integrated all these three types of fur into its coats of arms, along with coloured enamel and precious metals. Not every knight would have possessed such costly clothing; fur was now being imported from the most distant parts of the Orient by traders who were becoming more and more adventurous. Only the rich and powerful are portrayed in surviving documents, and little is known of less wealthy knights, who were probably attired in the fur of animals killed hunting, or domestic animals.

Fur had other uses besides the lining of courtly mantles. From the end of the twelfth century and the beginning of the thirteenth it was used to line and to edge the new style of headdress, the almuce, worn in court circles and later exclusively by clerics. The bonnet became much fuller, although still simple in shape, sometimes hanging half down the back, and it was fully lined with light fur. The chaperon was another variation on the hood and existed separately from the garment of which it had formerly been a part; it was more elaborate in cut and covered the head and shoulders closely. In the thirteenth century kings and courtiers adopted the habit of wearing a little linen coif tied under the chin; this could be worn on its own or under the hat or hood. This was not the full range of headgear. When summer arrived, makers of floral hats would sell plaited wreaths and, throughout the year, headpieces made of peacock feathers; knights also enjoyed trimming their headgear with pearl and gold circlets.

The shape of the clothing of the dominant classes does not appear to have altered very much over the twelfth and thirteenth centuries, but this may again be an impression based on insufficient documentation. Length and fullness varied slightly as the years passed, but this was sometimes connected with the function of the clothing. By contrast fabrics and decoration changed so greatly that the appearance of the clothing was transformed. The Crusades introduced the glamour and variety of textiles produced or used in the Islamic world to a large number of Western soldiers, but it was really the merchants who introduced fabrics made beyond the Mediterranean in increasing quantities. The Arab world competed with Byzantium in the export of all types of silk. Sheer silks (chiffon and crêpe), figured silks made in Damascus (hence 'damasks') and silk imported from India or China were particularly popular. The Middle East, Egypt and Sicily were not the only points of contact with the oriental textile tradition. Muslim Spain soon developed its own independent industry. The frontiers established by the Reconquest were not proof against the entry of merchandise from the East, and figured silk brocades were much in demand. Many Muslim craftsmen continued silk weaving in the areas recaptured by the Christian states. Some of the fabrics found in the royal tombs at Las Huelgas certainly originated in such workshops. Nevertheless, silk continued to be used mainly for ecclesiastical hangings and vestments.

The twelfth and particularly the thirteenth centuries were a golden age in the development of woollen fabrics in the West. Coloured woollen cloth was the princely fabric *par excellence*, especially in the regions farthest from the Mediterranean. Of course the climate made this necessary, but a cultural phenomenon like luxury clothing is not always governed by natural phenomena. The trade regulations that were now beginning to be written down reveal the processes of wool manufacturing in all their complexity. Archaeological finds have disclosed the many different aspects that wool could achieve: some of the wool is so fine and the spinning of such high quality that the resulting twill-weaves are as fine and as soft as silk. The thicker, felted wool gives outer garments and woollen cloaks the volume and hang that sculptors liked to depict. Frescoes, mosaics and even miniatures may not do full justice either to the colours of fabrics or to the contexts in which the clothes made from them were worn, but all the sources attest to the great strides being made in the art of dyeing and the new colours being produced. This was when blue made its first appearance and quickly became so popular in France that it was adopted by the king for his cloak and for his coat of arms. Green was obtained by mixing yellow with blue, yellow being the only colour that was little valued in the West. The high quality dark fabric known as 'brunette' was dyed first in a very concentrated bath of woad, followed by a dip in a bath of kermes. By now all the colours of the coat of arms were in place: the importance of coloured fabrics in the development of heraldry is self-evident. Late thirteenth-century chronicles emphasise the importance of colour in the courtier's appearance, in the glorification of his lineage and in the share of power inherited from it.

Medieval embroidery achieved a high level of perfection in the twelfth century with the work known as *opus anglicanum*, mainly known through the liturgical vestments that survive in museums and cathedrals. Late twelfth-century texts mention the custom of stitching coats of arms onto items of men's clothing, but it is not clear if the garments were intended for wearing at tournaments or if they were worn all the time at court; in the early fourteenth century chaperons began to bear elegantly embroidered coats of arms. Princes may have employed professional needlewomen, but nevertheless embroidery and silk ribbon weaving were activities considered suited to the rank of women of the nobility and often figure in the literature and poetry of chivalry. Embroidery must have been more widespread and put to more diverse uses than chronicles and royal ledgers suggest.

The belt became a very important fashion accessory at this time though, like embroidery, had significance that went beyond the purely decorative. As a symbolic protection to the person wearing it, the belt was a mark of 'virtue', courage combined with innocence. The belt was also used to hold daggers and other hand arms close to the body and was part of the military panoply reserved for members of the ruling class.

THE DEVELOPMENT OF ARMOUR

Armour, designed as protection for the combatant, was the distinctive badge of the warrior throughout the Middle Ages, initially being worn only by knights. The Roman breastplates that figure so prominently in Carolingian miniatures were replaced by a knee-length leather garment with short sleeves, the *broigne*, onto which 'mails' (metal plates or rings) were fixed. As protection for the neck and shoulders, knights also wore a metal hood or hauberk made of fine mail. When the tunic was made from similar links or rings of steel it was known as a 'coat of mail'; chain mail was suppler than the metal-plated tunic and, although more expensive, began gradually to be adopted by the chivalrous class. Armour made of metal plates was not abandoned completely. The jazerant mentioned in the *chansons de geste* was an armour made from metal plates linked by chain mail and, with few changes, it remained in use throughout the Middle Ages and beyond. At the end of the thirteenth century a new garment for protecting the upper part of the body came into fashion; this was made of horizontal steel strips fixed inside a covering of leather, canvas or linen and was called a 'brigandine'. The leather or canvas exterior hid the metal plates except for the bolts or rivets, which were often decorated. This piece of body armour remained in favour with men of the highest rank, for battle and for jousting, until the end of the Middle Ages. As protection for the arms and legs, but also the hands and feet, all of which were left unprotected by the sleeveless or short-sleeved coat of mail, various items made of chain mail with small links were worn: these could consist of flat panels laced behind the leg, or shaped like sheaths – the latter, like metal stockings, sometimes extended as high as the waist. The brigandine was shorter than the coat of mail and had to be worn with various metal accessories that protected the hips and stomach as well as the arms and legs. Steel plates shaped to fit the shins and thighs ('greaves' and 'cuisses') were strapped onto the chain mail leggings with straps of leather. The arms were covered in similar fashion with 'brassards' and elbow pieces, the hands with 'gauntlets' and the feet with 'solerets'.

It was also during the thirteenth century that the term *broigne* disappeared; suits of armour consisting of elements of hammered metal, of different shapes and sizes, were then called 'plates', the word 'brigandine' being reserved for the suits in which the horizontal metal strips were hidden inside. The use of rigid metal plates to protect certain parts of the body led eventually to the creation of whole suits of articulated metal plates known as 'plain harness'; these all-in-one armoured garments had to be made to measure by very skilled armourers. Because of their high cost they were accessible only to the wealthiest princes and knights. The protection they offered, however, was gained at the expense of agility. The big battles of the Hundred Years War demonstrated the vulnerability of a cavalry clothed in such heavy armour.

Protection of the head required all the improvements brought about by developments in metallurgy. In the Carolingian period the helmet was fashioned to the shape of the head; it did not cover very much and appears to have been formed from two halves joined by a metallic band that formed a crest. Then the shape changed and helmets became conical: a rare example of this style, dating from the eleventh century and unearthed in England, is constructed from segments joined and strengthened by vertical metal strips. As the Bayeux Tapestry illustrates, one of the metal strips would sometimes project downwards over the nose to protect the face; helmets of this description were worn for two centuries. At the end of the twelfth century the cylindrical saucepan-shaped helmet that covered the entire face made its appearance; this can be seen on effigies of warriors throughout the thirteenth century. From the thirteenth century the 'iron hat', consisting of a skullcap with a brim, can be seen on wax seals. In the fourteenth century the names and shapes of helmets began to diversify; the most important innovation was the invention of detachable and, later, hinged visors which allowed the face to be bared. The one-piece helmet was worn only for tournaments and jousting, and the crested helmets that had been worn in battle in the thirteenth century were now also worn only in tournaments. In the later Middle Ages

22 Georgius Zaparus: *Book of Astrology*. Bibliothèque Nationale, Paris, Lat.7330, f.7, illuminated in Sicily during the second quarter of the thirteenth century. The knight's head is protected by a helmet with a nasal (an extension protecting the nose). The armour consists of iron plates probably riveted to a leather undergarment.

armour would still be decorated, but the twelfth-century fashion for painted armour gave way to engraving, enamelling and especially gilding on helmets and bolts; if the chroniclers of the Duke of Burgundy are to be believed, headgear and even greaves were sometimes studded with rubies, pearls and diamonds.

THE INVENTION OF MODERN MASCULINE DRESS

Whatever their shape, a helmet and armour could not be worn over a straightforward linen shirt. Knights very soon adopted quilted clothing, worn as sole protection in battle by the infantry in the twelfth century, under their armour. This would be stuffed with cotton or hemp wadding and soon gained the name 'pourpoint' or doublet; the fabric, consisting of layers of fabric stitched together and then

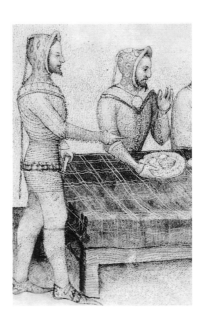

23   *Roman de Guiron Le Courtois.* Bibliothèque Nationale, Paris, Naf. 5243, f.50, illuminated in northern Italy in the last quarter of the fourteenth century. The doublet, a simple quilted garment, could be worn under the armour or other clothing, or on its own with hose.

stuffed with cotton (or silk) wadding, was made by specialised artisans. The new types of armour fitted the body closely, and these lining garments therefore had also to be close-fitting. The fitted sleeve with rounded top was invented to replace the usual T-shaped sleeve, which required elongation of the shoulders. The T-sleeve, which had to be wide and always crumpled under the arms when the arm was lowered, was unwearable under the brigandine, and even more so under the full harness. It became the custom to line some of the pieces of armour with leather or fabric, or even with strips or cushions of padding. The legs were protected by leggings of fine linen or wool which were attached at the top to the doublet.

Royal and princely account books show that, from the thirteenth century on, the outfits worn under armour were made of expensive fabrics: hose of fine wool, and pourpoints of figured silk or embroidered velvet. The information gleaned from these ledgers suggests that these garments may have been worn on their own in the intimacy of private apartments, or in a tent on the battlefield, but there is no other written or pictorial evidence to support this. It is only towards the end of the 1330s that chroniclers throughout Europe remark with some indignation about young soldiers disporting themselves in public in clothes that hug the figure quite so closely. Some

24   Guillaume de Lorris and Jean de Meung: *Roman de la Rose*. Bibliothèque Nationale, Paris, Fr. 1567, f.7, fourteenth century. During the second half of the fourteenth century men wore their short, fitted costumes decorated with buttons, low belts and long, dangling elbow pieces; their *chaperons* and attached capes becoming increasingly important.

said the fashion came from Italy, some from France, but all said it came from another country: whatever the truth of the matter the opportunity to grumble (once again) about the moral decay evidenced by such clothes could not be missed, nor, for clerics as well as for members of the emerging bourgeoisie, the opportunity to inveigh against the rowdiest members of a class whose dominance and showy wealth were becoming increasingly intolerable.

For many costume historians the middle of the fourteenth century marks the beginning of fashion as a phenomenon; the new way of dressing represented fashion that imposed its taste and its rhythms on a restricted social class. Estimates of the duration of fashions in clothing show movement on two levels: the details were in a constant state of change, while big modifications of the silhouette took place only about every fifty years. The iconography surviving for the period before the fourteenth century is not sufficient to provide a continuous picture of developments in costume; but the detailed descriptions left by some of the chroniclers imply that sweeping changes and extraordinary (sometimes unwelcome) innovations had taken place beforehand.

COURT FASHIONS AND FIGURES

From the thirteenth century onwards, and particularly in the four-teenth and fifteenth centuries, sources of information become more numerous: surviving documents describe the clothing made for princes and their entourage; the materials are listed in detail, as are the colours; the people for whom the garments were being made are identified; and sometimes even the feast days or entertainments for which they were intended are also included. Such lists allow one to guess at the rivalries that existed within each court, and at the com-petition between different courts on the occasion of visiting royalty, royal weddings or diplomatic missions from abroad. Images and sculpture from the mid-fourteenth century onwards show a new con-cern for realism which serves to illustrate and emphasise the diversity in modes of dress. The small amount of extant clothing and more numerous fragments from archaeological digs provide accurate, detailed information about the way clothes were made. On the other hand, the much fuller documentary evidence raises all sorts of prob-lems for collectors and collators of data: the substitution of the ver-nacular for Latin and the use of words with scant relationship to Latin, plus the borrowing of terms from one vernacular language to another. The proliferation of terminology occurred in response to an outburst of creativity in styles of design, the advent of all sorts of new materials and the increasing significance of colour.

The masculine overgarment changed its shape and name less fre-quently than other items of clothing. In the fifteenth century, for example, the mantle was also called 'sack', a word that was probably Byzantine in origin and transmitted via the German *Sack*. The func-tions of the mantle survived unaltered – it not only provided warmth and protection but served as a symbol of dignity and prestige. Variations were only in length and fullness, according to the different purposes to which it might be put. The same could be said of the undergarments, particularly those not exposed to view and purely functional in use. The *braies* were made of fine linen or cotton or, for comfort on horseback, chamois leather. Shirts, which were invisible until the mid-fifteenth century, varied only in the quality of the fab-ric used, usually fine linen. Later they were embellished with silk embroidery, pearl buttons and so on. The pourpoint survived unchanged in name or in shape throughout the period under consid-eration. According to whether it was intended to be worn under armour or in civilian life, hidden or exposed, its material would be more or less expensive and its cut and detailing more or less elaborate. In an aristocratic or princely environment this was the first garment regularly to be made of silk and decorated with embroidery. In the fourteenth century the doublet usually buttoned right down the front, whereas in the fifteenth century lacing was introduced, tight to start with, then later across a wide V-neck that allowed the shirt to show through. Like the doublet, hose could be either hidden under long garments or exposed if worn with very short clothing. As some of the trade regulations applying to hosiers show, hose were already cut on the bias in the thirteenth century; they were at first fastened by laces attached under the basque, then, after about 1380, by 'aglets', unattached laces made of silk or leather with little metal tags at each end, gold or silver for royalty, gilded copper for less extravagant attire. When much shorter doublets became the fashion, the material for each leg would be stitched together at the top for the sake of decency, thus forming 'joined hose' (tights).

In spite of the stir that accompanied the novelty of figure-hugging male attire, the earlier mode of dress was not abandoned immediately or completely. The *robe*, meaning a collection of matching layered garments made of the same material, remained the basic item of aristocratic and princely clothing until the last thirty years of the fourteenth century. The names given to the various elements of the *robe* vary, as do the number of pieces, always fewer for ceremonial dress made from costly silks and consisting of only one or two tunics and a cloak. The woollen winter clothing of people of the highest rank could usually be broken down into four to six elements, at least some of them lined with fur (the surcoat, mantle, *housse* and sometimes the *chaperon*), the others with fabric (the *cotte* or *garde-corps*). It seems likely that individual garments were worn separately more and more frequently. Younger people regarded the mantle and hood as belonging to the new fashion. During the third quarter of the fourteenth century young knights and squires are often portrayed wearing a *jaque* or jerkin, a fitted garment, usually mid-thigh in length – longer than a doublet. Fashion now required a longer silhouette with a pronounced bulging of the chest, obtained by padding. The garment known as Charles de Blois' doublet, which dates from 1364, shows how the bulge was accentuated by buttons from top to bottom, spherical ones on the chest and flat ones on the waist and hips.

With this type of garment, buttons became an important feature of masculine attire. They were sometimes made of the same material as the doublet or jacket, but also occasionally made of gold. Precious metals were cast or chased, enriched with real or imitation gems, or sometimes decorated with niello or coloured enamel. Decorations frequently included plant or animal motifs, letters and pious or amorous inscriptions; the same type of designs were used on belts and buckles.

In the second half of the fourteenth century wide, heavy belts made of hinged metal sections were popular; these were worn on the hips over short, civilian clothing as well as over armour. They might be embellished with stamped or enamelled designs, or gemstones, genuine or fake. The fashion for leather or silk belts decorated with buckles and clasps and metal panels, sometimes studded with pearls and other stones, lasted for a long time; it is easy to imagine that, at some courts, the belts would be hung with detachable items – papers and letters, little bells etc. Purses were suspended from the belt too, sometimes a small gathered purse on a metal frame and sometimes just a flat pocket. Arms also hung from the belt, a dagger stuck into the flat purse or a sword supported at the top by a baldric. Great attention was paid to the pommel and the scabbard. The carrying of weapons was no longer reserved for members of the chivalrous class, and so a knight would have to demonstrate his superiority by the glamour and high quality of his small arms.

With the advent of new, short clothing, the garments comprising the *robe* disappeared in the last quarter of the fourteenth century. Sleeved outer garments – the *cotte*, surcoat, *garde-corps* and mantle – were supplanted by a hybrid garment, the *houppelande*, distinguishable from its predecessors mainly by its front opening, from top to bottom. Initially it was the fashion for the *houppelande* to be all-enveloping. It was worn over doublet and hose, or over a *cotta*, and had a high collar. The wide sleeves were gathered on the shoulder and sometimes hung down to the ground. It could be worn full-length or to mid-calf or mid-thigh. The *haincelin*, a shorter version of the *houppelande*, was named after Charles vi of France's court jester, Haincelin Coq, and shows just how important the royal courts were in launching new fashions in dress, especially when the king was a young man. The *houppelande* was a luxurious garment, often styled and decorated in exquisite detail. The hems and sleeves could be scalloped or dagged in fancy shapes (such as leaves), or had appliqués in contrasting colours stitched on, or they might be edged with fur. The slashes cut in the skirt and sleeves were lined in the same way; when the fashion for tight cuffs returned, the slits were used as openings for the arms so that the sleeves of the doublet could be displayed. This explains why pourpoints were often made from two different fabrics, the costlier of the two being reserved for the sleeves. The *houppelande* could be worn open like a sleeved mantle, or belted, and was often lined with fur.

During the first half of the fifteenth century the name *houppelande* gradually disappeared from the court ledgers, to be replaced by the word *robe*, now used to describe a type of gown rather than a collection of garments. The *robe* would be long for ceremonial wear and short for every day; while retaining a fullness characteristic of the early part of the century, this aspect was more carefully controlled. On gowns with accentuated shoulders the sleeves continued to be wide. Unpressed, symmetrical pleats, stitched horizontally across the chest, gave fullness above a naturally tailored waist. The cut and ornamentation became less extreme towards the mid-fifteenth century. Figured materials were preferred to embroidery and scallops. Fur was used less liberally and now was usually confined to a broad band along the lower hem of a garment, long or short.

The doublet and hose constituted the basic elements of the masculine wardrobe from now on, but with different overgarments. The short-sleeved paletot, with open seams under the arms, and the *huque*, cut in the same way but more gathered, first appeared in Italy and then spread throughout the West.

Hats and headgear kept pace with the changing silhouette, sometimes emphasising it. With the short, fitted clothing of the fourteenth century the hood covered the head and shoulders, leaving just the face peeping through the opening. The *cornette* or point of the *chaperon*, an elongated version of the early hood, hung right down the back, so long that it was sometimes tucked into the belt or wrapped around the head. With the *houppelande* it became habitual for the wearer to pull the side and shoulder pieces of the hood on top of the head and tie them with the point. Before long the hood was being worn like a hat. By the middle of the fifteenth century it had grown greatly in size and was constructed on a thick circular roll. Hats grew larger at this time as well. Felt hats began to have crowns that widened at the top, and the wide-brimmed beaver was very popular. Bonnets and birettas grew to such a size that they exceeded the height of the face. It was general practice to trim the headgear with embroidery and ribbons in gold and silk; brooches were used to fasten peacock and ostrich feathers to the brim.

Once short clothing had become fashionable in the mid-fourteenth century shoes were on view and their shape changed quite radically. The long, tapering 'poulaines', echoing the narrow, stretched look of the rest of the dress at the time, came back into fashion, on riding boots as well as on lighter shoes. Before this, shoes had generally been ankle-high, and fastened with laces or thongs. In the second half of the fourteenth century a style of highly decorated cutwork sandal was introduced. There are many examples of these in contemporary paintings and the examples found in the London excavations show how many different techniques were used in their creation – openwork, engraving, stamping and printing, embroidery. Towards the end of the century well-dressed townsfolk were beginning to wear overshoes to protect their hose or delicate shoes; these consisted of thick wooden or cork soles held on by a strap. The examples found in London show that the strap was sometimes painted and that the wooden soles were occasionally made from two halves joined together.

This fashion for tightness and elongation in clothing and accessories remained in favour until the last decades of the fifteenth century. Sooner or later, according to area, the tendency was reversed: a preference developed for gowns without waists, opening from square rather than fitted shoulders, for large, flat hats, and for shoes shaped like ducks' bills, all of which heralded the fashions of the Renaissance.

FABRICS AND COLOURS

Fluctuations in the general outline of costume were accompanied, until the end of the Middle Ages, by equally significant fluctuations in the choice of materials, colours and ornamentation. At the end of the thirteenth century and beginning of the fourteenth silk was used mainly for the doublets and surcoats worn on their own or under armour, probably mainly for tournaments. These garments did not require a lot of fabric but they were embellished with silk and gold thread embroidery which, according to Joinville's *Vie de Saint Louis* (1309), betrayed a new addiction to luxury; Joinville compares this extravagant ornamentation to the simpler fashions current at the time of Louis IX, when gold leaf was roughly tacked to the fabric. Only ceremonial vestments worn at royal coronations or marriages required such costly materials. The garments comprising a suit were generally made of woollen fabric, the quality and colour of which varied according to whether they were intended for court life or for travel and horsemanship.

Scarlets, preferably dyed dark red and purple, were important items in the wardrobes of kings and princes, but perse (blue-green) and azure fabrics, dyed in woad, also figured and were more common than straightforward greens; blue fabrics were sometimes decorated with red or grey stripes, or narrow vermilion streaks. Multi-coloured wool fabrics were popular too, chequered wool and mixtures remaining in fashion for years. Brunette was the only dark woollen fabric that was appreciated. At this period yellow wool began to be worn in courtly circles. Princes loved bright colours and enjoyed wearing bold quarters of contrasting fabrics on the same garment. For example, the Comte d'Artois, grandson of and also brother-in-law of a king, combined scarlet with a peach-coloured wool, a yellow with a blue striped with red, and a striped stuff to contrast with white wool. Clothes in plain colours were often lined with contrasting fabrics or furs. Vair was reserved for silk or costly scarlet; other woollen fabrics were lined with less expensive furs like lamb or squirrel. Light silks dyed black, green or red were preferred for lining clothes less warmly.

Tastes in fabrics, colours and furs changed only slowly during the fourteenth century. Wool remained paramount in the costume of princes and knights, though silk was beginning to gain ground for small garments like doublets and hoods. The lists contained in royal inventories prove that silk robes were still considered to be the most prized possessions of a prince. Some of the robes described in detail were covered in gold-thread or silk embroidery, with pearls and other stones stitched all over them, and were real treasures.

Where did the fashion for black that arrived at the end of the fourteenth century come from? Was it the invention of an individual or group of people wanting to make themselves conspicuous by wearing the direct opposite of the gaudy colours worn by others in their entourage? If that was the case, it would only have speeded up a development already heralded by progress in fabric production, particularly in dyeing. The very few woollen fabrics mentioned in the archives of the Tuscan merchant Francesco Datini prove that very concentrated colours were obtainable by this time, and that the green

25   *Triptych of Jan de Witte* (detail). Musées Royaux des Beaux-Arts, Brussels,
1473. Black became popular after the end of the fourteenth century, particularly
among the aristocracy. The gentleman's *houppelande* and lady's gown depicted
here are made of fine black silk, his lined with dark fur and hers with light fur.

and peacock blue on sale were very dark. It seems likely, therefore,
that black silks originated in Italy; the fashion for black entered the
courts in the form of silk garments and was to remain there. The
sumptuary laws enacted by the authorities of a number of Italian
towns had their part to play in this process. In order to preserve the
distance between the nobility and the *nouveaux riches*, who could now
afford to dress in silk, one of the recurrent edicts prohibited non-aris-
tocrats from wearing silk of any colour except black. Production of
dark fabrics must have increased, and the search for quality been stimulated by the demands of this wealthy clientèle. The new fabrics that
arrived on the market attracted the aristocracy north of the Alps by
their originality; these members of the nobility probably knew
nothing of the discriminatory significance that black fabrics had
acquired in their country of origin.

The type of clothing made from black silks evidently followed the latest fashion: they were nearly always made into doublets and *houppelandes*. The fashion was by no means transitory: in the late fourteenth century and throughout the fifteenth Western princes and aristocrats displayed a definite taste for black. The Duke of Burgundy, Philip the Good, was perhaps an extreme case; according to his chroniclers he wore only black, as a sign of mourning, after the assassination of his father, John the Fearless, in 1419. Portraits of him show outfits of the greatest elegance that provide an admirable foil for his jewellery. Black was not always worn with such rigour of purpose. The fabrics were often brocaded – damask, satin, figured velvet. Those in a single colour would exploit the contrast between matt and shiny patterns, while polychrome fabrics would play black against bright colours. 'Cloth of gold' contrasted shining metallic threads with black. Like woollen clothes, black silk clothing was often lined with bright colours, more easily visible since the arrival of the *houppelande*, the masculine version of which opened down the front. During the late fourteenth century and the first half of the fifteenth clothing was very highly ornamented: embroidery would be accompanied by metallic figures stitched to the fabric. Fixed or mobile spangles, hanging from little rings, or small pieces of jewellery sometimes studded with coloured gemstones would embellish the *houppelande*, the hood and even the hose.

The fashion for dark furs appeared at the same time as that for dark silks and was not restricted to black. Sable, black in terms of heraldry, is a dark, glowing brown with subtle nuances of colour; civet cat is dark grey with paler highlights; and squirrel, like beaver, is brown. The only truly black skins belong to lambs, and these were appreciated by princes from about the 1420s; the most sought-after of these were of the quality of astrakhan. Dark furs made much less impact than dark silks because fur was seldom used on the outside of a garment. Fur increased the volume of clothing and emphasised any openings or slashes, but did not determine the overall colour scheme. In the late fourteenth century inventories of the wardrobe of King Richard II of England show that in London fur accompanied velvet, satin and black brocade, but also crimson and blue silk and scarlet wool. At the Burgundian court, whose luxury and extravagance exercised a powerful influence for nearly a century, fabrics continued to appear in a wide range of colours. Although fur was displayed with discretion in male attire, its use reached unprecedented levels in

Western courts at the end of the fourteenth century, to decline slowly but inexorably in the fifteenth. Few could afford the immensely high cost of fur, which therefore came to be a symbol of the greatest extravagance. The value of the fur was often greater than the value of the fabric it was used to line; only in gowns made of 'cloth of gold' did the price of the fabric equal that of the Prussian sable lining. Both of these materials immediately classified the wearer as being at the summit of the hierarchy of power, expressed in terms of such display of wealth.

Meetings between courts gave their leaders a useful opportunity to flaunt their dignity. Even a prince with austere tastes like the Comte de Savoie, normally satisfied with clothing in monochrome colours, white and grey, with furs in the same shades, procured for himself on the occasion of the marriage of his sister to the Duke of Bavaria in 1445 the purple velvets and sables that were fitting to his rank. Richer by far than many kings, the Dukes of Burgundy were masters of the art of dressing extravagantly in order to display their power. The pains taken by the Burgundian chroniclers to re-create the splendour and organisation of the many ceremonials, particularly tournaments, put on by the Dukes of Burgundy, is revealing. The same concern emerges from the descriptions written by their rival and political adversay, René d'Anjou, and the members of his entourage, to retain the memory of the parades, jousts and tournaments held at his court. In these accounts the ostentation receives far more attention than valour and weaponry. Descriptions of the finery worn for the march-past of combatants, then of the new outfits donned for the ball at the end of the day, take up much more space than accounts of assaults and their outcome. Fashion and extravagance had overrun a province where previously a certain simplicity had been the order of the day. At the beginning of the fifteenth century the vestments worn over armour, and the housings worn by the horses, were still made of woollen cloth or thick cotton decorated with gold tinsel and paint. From 1440 onwards there are extremely detailed descriptions that itemise a whole collection of fabrics, each more expensive than the last: cloth of gold, velvets, brocaded satins. The ornaments were as costly, gaudy and noisy as can be imagined: trinkets of gold and jewellery, bells and jingling trinkets. The parody of fashion included the use of the costliest furs as edgings to the knight's coats of arms as well as the horses' housings and harnesses; only ermine, genette (civet cat) and sable were good enough. Heraldic devices gave way to imaginary

26 *Codex Manesse*. Universitätsbibliothek, Heidelberg, Cod. Pal. Germ. 848, f.82v, *c*. 1330. Von Limbourg bequest. Before taking part in a tournament, the knight is attired in a coat of arms bearing a motif that is different from the one on his horse's housing. Here he is receiving, from the hands of his lady, a helmet adorned with a crest of peacock feathers.

decorative motifs, often borrowed from the convoluted symbolism of courtly literature or pastoral. Towards the end of the Hundred Years War, knights of the highest rank were prepared to take part in a tournament or to break lances that were covered in 'teardrops', roses, trifles, or the pastoral accessories of the stage shepherd – crook, pipe etc – all embroidered in gold thread. Clothing bearing the coats of arms of the jousters was less common in reality than the history of heraldry would have us believe.

Helmet crests, worn only for tournaments and jousting after the fourteenth century, underwent the same process of evolution. In

Germanic countries they remained hereditary emblems in the same way as the armorials, but in other areas they became the emblem of an individual. Like the coats of arms for men and horses they could be changed at each encounter. Made of light materials like wood and soft leather, they usually consisted of a central face piece with a 'flight' of plumes on either side. The top of the helmet was sometimes wrapped round with fabric which floated out behind. In the centre of this structure would be a heraldic device, or an imaginary man or beast, a human head, a fruit, a tool or even a whole scene with figures. Like the 'devices' themselves (phrases expressing thoughts in a deliberately enigmatic way, much prized in courtly circles), crests hovered somewhere between the real and the imaginary. The clothing accompanying the crests affirmed their wearer's membership of the ruling class, endorsing his position in society and his power by the display of fabrics and furs, the variety of forms and decoration and the brilliance of the gold and the colours.

CHAPTER SIX

The Diffusion and Regulation of Fashion

FROM MASCULINE TO FEMININE FASHION

The detached attitude generally adopted by men in the nineteenth and twentieth centuries towards their clothing contrasts sharply with that of the princes and courtiers of the Middle Ages, whose role in the creation and diffusion of fashion was of critical importance. Bearing in mind later developments, and also the accusations brought against women by the mysogynist tradition of medieval literature, the subordinate role played in the spread of fashions by women of the ruling classes is often admitted only reluctantly. Of course, the immense imbalance in the documentation of the period might be cited as an excuse: queens and women of the aristocracy appear much less frequently in the chroniclers' narratives than do rulers and warriors, and the iconography contains few female figures, at least before the thirteenth century. When written documents, particularly the royal account books, become sufficiently detailed and plentiful to allow comparisons to be made, it turns out that expenditure by queens and princesses on their clothing is, in general, lower than that of their menfolk; their purchases are less frequent and less varied. When the given data make comparison possible, it is confirmed that a garment or an outfit made for a princess almost always cost less than the equivalent made for a man of equal rank. There are exceptions, of course, like the Duke of Savoy who, in the early fifteenth century, dressed very simply for daily life. At ceremonial occasions, on the other hand, when he was on parade with other princes, he wore the fabrics and furs appropriate to his rank. Generally speaking, the role played by princesses in the development of the luxury that accompanied the growth of fashion in medieval court circles appears to have been a secondary one; this would be consonant anyway with medieval notions of the superiority of men over women.

Chroniclers have little to say about female fashion and its changes. They occasionally mention luxurious fabrics and finery, but the

27   *Vie de Sainte Radegonde*. Bibliothèque Municipale, Poitiers, MS 250, f. 22v,
illuminated in Poitiers in the third quarter of the eleventh century. The women
are wearing a tunic with wide-bottomed sleeves over a shift with fitted sleeves.
Their head is entirely covered with a veil, which conceals their hair – symbol of
feminine seductiveness.

gem-studded headbands and mantles of silk and jacinth attributed to
the daughters of Charlemagne are probably simply poetic licence.
Carolingian miniatures are highly stylised; they show women dressed
in long robes with their heads covered by a veil that sometimes
covers them completely, in the timeless fashion that aims at conceal-
ing the hair, a symbol of female seduction. This was the appearance
authorised by the church; the narratives, however, paint quite a different picture of secular life. Queens adorn themselves with ribbons
and glamorous girdles, permitting themselves extravagances such as
shoes with long, long points favoured by Queen Irmentrude, wife of
Charles the Bald, in the ninth century. A little later the veil began to
be worn as a cloak over a long gown with decorated borders. From
the eleventh century onwards a *bliand* (over-tunic) was worn over
another, sometimes longer, gown a *chainse* which itself was worn
over a linen chemise. The fashion for long, flowing garments that
was alleged to give the men who wore them an effeminate appearance had no noticeable influence on women's apparel, except possibly on the exaggerated width of the sleeves; around the middle of the
twelfth century these hung so low that they had to be knotted to

prevent them dragging on the floor. As was freqently the case, fashion affected only one feature of female attire; any more radical modification of the silhouette would have encountered too many prohibitions.

Sleeves and headdresses were particularly favoured aspects of women's clothing. Veils became more modest in the thirteenth century; still worn to envelop the head and shoulders, they were now made of finer fabric and were often held in place by a broad linen band or a cylindrical *touret* of a shape reminiscent of the masculine brimmed cap. In the fourteenth century divergences between male and female fashion became more pronounced. There would have been no question of a woman adopting the two-piece male outfit that revealed the legs so generously. The feminine version of this innovation was manifest in gowns with close-fitting sleeves and bodices – enhanced by a large number of small ornamental buttons – the round décolleté over the shoulders and the opening of the overdress to hip level under the arms. The headdress began to shed its floating veils and wimples and was sometimes reduced to a simple circlet made of jewellery, ribbons or flowers, worn over plaited hair dressed to frame the face. For outdoor wear a hood would generally be worn; the female hood, unlike the version for men, buttoned under the chin but was often worn open.

No rule of propriety stood in the way of ladies' adopting the flowing *houppelande*; the same dagging and decorations, the same full or slashed sleeves were worn by both sexes. The women's model continued to be closed down the front, even though it was worn over other long garments; by way of compensation, perhaps, it developed a train, sometimes a very long one. It was in the choice of materials that the difference between men's and women's clothing is clearest. At the end of the fourteenth century black (in either silk or fur) failed to seduce princesses as much as it had kings and knights. Women rejected dark fur almost unanimously: miniver, ermine, white Russian weasel and even white lamb remained in favour. Black silk fabrics exerted a little more pull, but only gradually; velvets became popular, particularly for accessories.

While men always wore a hood with the *houppelande*, women only occasionally did so. Soon, however, much more voluminous headdresses, built up on a padded *bourrelet*, came into fashion. These developed vertically and gave rise to some amazing creations, some spherical and some cylindrical, or even split into two like horns: they

28   *Histoire de Charles Martel*. Bibliothèque Royale Albert Ier, Brussels, MS 7, f.59v, illuminated in Flanders by Loyset Liédet, *c.*1470. From 1430 onwards women of the aristocracy took to wearing conical, increasingly tall, headdresses; these were known as *hennins*.

elicited biting sarcasm and censure from moralists and priests. Scorn was also poured on the *hennin* that appeared in about 1430; this consisted of a conical headpiece with a veil attached to the point, the veil either fluttering loose or forming pleats or wings, held in place by a large number of pins.

The *houppelande* was abandoned at about this period. Princesses rediscovered gowns with close-fitting sleeves and bodices whose V–necklines were edged with fur. Although the silhouette was elongated by the high headdresses and trains, the difference between male and female attire now grew more entrenched: men's fashion exaggerated the width of the shoulders and the slenderness of the waist and showed off the legs; women wore gowns with narrow shoulders and tight bodices, belted above or just below the waistline, the fullness of

29   Georges de Chasteaulens: *Dream*. Musée Condé, Chantilly, MS 498 (1569), illuminated in France in the fifteenth century. In the fifteenth century female headgear developed some extraordinary constructions. Held up with pins and fine brass wire, the starched veil hung like flowing wings.

their garments extending from the hips. By somewhere between 1480 and 1490 the vertical style had been largely abandoned; the characteristic features of men's fashion had no female equivalent. Nevertheless there were queens, princesses or mistresses who liked to compete with male monarchs in procuring the same amount (or more) of jewellery, cloth of gold and pale silks, not forgetting the costly furs – though these were used with moderation. Female costume offered no competition to the strength expressed by the broad padded shoulders of male garb, nor to the freedom of movement permitted to the legs on display below the full, short, open robes. The distinction between the male and female silhouette was growing.

ECONOMY AND ECONOMICS

An obstacle of quite a different nature stood in the way of the diffusion of fashions beyond the close-knit circle of kings and queens and the wealthier members of their entourage, and it was connected with economy rather than with ideology. In fact if the revenues of a duke and a count had no common measure, then those of a king and the knights in his entourage had even less. Fashionable fabrics and furs cost a fortune and needed constant renewal; almost none of the courtiers would have been able to afford life at court without assistance. The prince's favour conferred largesse, whether financial or in clothing and fabrics. Only in exceptional circumstances, nevertheless, would the courtiers have figured as beneficiaries of garments as sumptuous as those of their ruler, a privilege reserved for members of the family. The allocation of coats of arms and horse's housings worn at a tournament certainly permitted the squires to obtain opulent fabrics, but such a windfall was far from frequent and had to be shared. The distribution to the menservants of 'common clothing', a proportion of which they would probably sell, was a likely way of disseminating innovations in fashion, at least innovations in shape, cut and detail.

Only in the romances of the Knights of the Round Table was the company of knights a society of equals. In real life, fortune did not smile equally on those at court, and the literary theme of the 'abused at court' who met financial ruin through trying to emulate the clothing of his peers must have mirrored the experience of many a courtier lacking private means. The authorities have, throughout history, attempted to regulate expenditure in the face of such temptation. In Ancient Rome a law was drawn up designed to curb expenditure on clothing in times of war. About 808 a law passed by Charlemagne set the price of clothing; it is not clear, in fact, if this was in an effort to limit spending on dress or simply an exchange control mechanism. Later regulations and laws are much easier to interpret. Economic reasons are often cited, and these apply at two levels. From the ruler's point of view, fear of capital leaving the principality was the motive behind measures to curb the import of expensive fabrics from abroad. Import control also helped to encourage local industry. This was certainly the aim of the first English sumptuary law, passed in 1337, which prohibited the wearing of fabrics not woven in England. From the point of view of the domestic economy, it was to the sovereign's advantage to prevent the impoverishment of families, especially of those that constituted his army, or trained and armed it partially at their own expense. This preoccupation can be sensed in the first sumptuary laws imposed in the West, the laws drawn up by Philip the Fair, which aimed at relating to their income the quantity and quality of the clothing bought annually by members of the nobility. Under such strictures it became almost impossible to follow fashions which, in court circles, required enormously costly materials.

Certain ingenious practices, it is true, allowed luxurious items to be imitated at a fraction of the price. Even on princes' vestments ermine was occasionally replaced by less scarce white fur, spotted with black lamb's wool. Yellow silk threads lent figured silks the aspect of cloth of gold. Fabrics mixed with silk, or with wool, were also an attempt to create an illusion. Jewellery and accessories used silver-gilt and bronze-gilt. Trade regulations for a long time banned belt clasps and buckles made of tin because the metal looked too like silver when it was polished; archaeological finds prove nevertheless that these were common in the second half of the fourteenth century. In a society acutely aware of visual messages, eyes must have been practised at distinguishing fakes and imitations; the illusion of luxury was constantly sought after all the same.

SOCIAL ORDER, MORAL ORDER AND THE REGULATION OF APPEARANCES

In fact, the choice of a 'look' was only partly dependent on economic circumstances. Payment of the tailor and cutter contributed little to the cost of any garment, and people continued to make use of the services of the most skilled tailors or doublet makers. Most of those in receipt of liveries or of gifts of fabric had no access to the services of the prince's craftsmen. The arguments used in support of the sumptuary laws invoked the necessity of maintaining a strictly hierarchical social order more often than they invoked economic necessity. In the great kingdoms as well as the independent city-states ruled by an aristocracy keen to hold on to its social status, the laws were an attempt to emphasise and reinforce the differences between the categories they defined more or less accurately. The most illustrative surviving example of this is contained in the Statutes of Savoy, laid down in 1430 by Duke Amadeus VIII. Book V, concerning 'moderation of the superfluous', defines no fewer than thirty-nine categories of people, from the reigning duke to the unmarried daughters of peasants and other labourers. More than half the groups identified belong to the nobility, although the sumptuary laws usually limit themselves to establishing the distinction between nobles and non-nobles.

Members of the ducal family are divided into five tiers, of which the duke and duchess occupy the first two. Nothing is prohibited to them, although they are cautioned to avoid clothing that is too luxurious; a limit is set on the length of the duchess's train. Their sons are recommended to wear garments shorter than their father's, and they are forbidden to wear gold until they have been dubbed knights.

Throughout the layers of this table of Savoyard society the rank of wives and their unmarried daughters is always subordinate to that of their respective husbands or fathers, but their classification is much simpler than that of the males. As far down as the fifteenth tier, birth is the sole criterion. The only personally acquired title that might influence the placing of a nobleman is that of 'doctor'. Among the non-nobles, categories twenty to twenty-nine relate to doctors, lawyers, university graduates, administrators in the duke's entourage and their wives and unmarried daughters. For each group, the cut and ornamentation of clothing and the value of the fabrics are all regulated. For example, the duke decides on the length of his secretaries' robes; they should not be above the knee or below the ankle. The use of fabrics is strictly hierarchical: woollen cloth depends on price per ell, and colour. The employment of silk is less tightly controlled in the Savoy Statutes than in contemporary regulations from the German countries, the British Isles or France, and for obvious reasons: Piedmont, close to the Italian silk-producing centres, was united with the Duchy of Savoy the previous year.

The regulations are more stringent for the ten categories below the nobility and for the holders of university or ducal positions. Scarlet is forbidden to the bourgeoisie and to tradesmen, even to those living on unearned income. In similar vein artisans are forbidden to wear long, pointed shoes or high-heeled boots, while peasants and manual labourers are prohibited from wearing clothes made of two different fabrics, slashed or scalloped garments; their robes must be made from cheap fabrics, but they are permitted to buy something of a slightly better quality for the hood.

This description of the social order by a fifteenth-century prince can be compared with the information provided by the account books of his court. The eldest son, heir to Duke Amadeus, author of the Statutes of Savoy, is favoured far above his brothers and sisters. On the occasion of a marriage, cloth of gold, satin, crimson damask and even purple velvet are all issued to him, whereas his siblings (the brothers being still too young to be knights) have to make do with

30   Albucasis: *Tacuinum Sanitatis*. Bibliothèque Nationale,
Paris, Nal. 1673, f.66, illuminated in Lombardy *c.*
1390–1400. The clothes worn by the merchant and those of
the poor man buying from him are quite different. The
quality and amount of fabric, the colours and also the number
of garments worn suggest a clear-cut hierarchy.

much less. The allocation of livery at the court of Savoy, as in other
princely courts, underlined the complex gradations of status that the
prince hoped to see reflected in the costume of his entourage. Some
of the criteria for differentiation set out in the Statutes of Savoy, such
as the cut, ornamentation or length of clothes, are omitted from the
account books; but all the documents confirm the distinctions based
on the type of cloth chosen, its value, its colour and the yardage
granted to each person.

Contemporary kings and princes must have had a view of the social
hierarchy that was similar to that of Amadeus of Savoy, as their personal purchases and their distribution of liveries or gifts of clothing
show. On the other hand, it is not safe to assume that they shared the
moral scruples of the Duke of Savoy where sumptuary expenditure

was concerned. In fact, the Statutes were not primarily intended to make hierarchical divisions according to expenditure on clothing and other outward displays of wealth. The first version of 1403 does not even mention such an aim; it claims emphatically to be defending the standards of Christian morality by denouncing transgressions that might arouse the wrath of God and cause plague and other miseries. This religious fear and the call to repentance and to the abandonment of reprehensible practices such as drinking alcohol, playing dice, dancing, or family celebrations can be found in quite a number of the urban sumptuary laws of the German Empire. The influence of public preaching, particularly by the mendicant orders, can be clearly sensed. Fifteenth-century chroniclers describe scenes following public sermons in more than one town, during which clothing and other items of dress that have attracted censure are publicly burnt.

Combining moral, hierarchical and economic issues with the regulation of expenditure (particularly on clothing), statutes developed in the late thirteenth century in the towns of Italy and also in large towns near the Mediterranean coastline, in Provence, Languedoc and Catalonia. The principal reason for their emergence was economic growth in these regions and the enrichment of certain categories of town dwellers. Much later, in fact not until the fifteenth century, the rapid progress of German towns elicited the same response. Here, as in the royal and princely decrees, the main explanation for the social classification sought by the authorities in legislation on clothing was to distinguish the nobility fron the non-nobility. The hierarchical tiers were more or less the same everywhere, and there would often be instructions for peasants outside the town as well. Sartorial signs were also used to distinguish people outside the boundaries of society – heretics, Jews, prostitutes and sometimes beggars. No other set of regulations, however, can rival the Statutes of Savoy in the detailed stratification of urban society.

TOWN DOUBLETS AND COUNTRY DOUBLETS

The extent to which individuals conformed to the sumptuary laws can be gleaned from wills and testaments, account books and inventories, which give the overwhelming impression that most people had only the bare necessities in their wardrobe and were not in a position to be influenced by the fashions worn by their social superiors. Any position at court, no matter how modest, carried a dispensation from the general rule, however. There was a law in England expressly drawn up to cover this practice, also borne out in the inventories of the retinue of the Dukes of Burgundy, now in Dijon. During the closing years of the fourteenth century silk makes a discreet appearance among the clothing listed, usually in the form of linings or sleeves, occasionally as a doublet. The fact that certain townsfolk unconnected to the court wore silk doublets testifies to the slightly blurred borderline between nobility and non-nobility: for example, a wealthy apothecary, married to a young lady of the minor nobility, allowed himself the luxury of a silk doublet, whereas other citizens with just as much money made do with cloth or fustian. Written evidence shows incontrovertibly that the new fashion was adopted by the wealthier denizens of Dijon in the late fourteenth century, although this is apparently at variance with the iconography that portrays citizens in long or calf-length gowns. In fact, the doublets made of ordinary fabrics mentioned in the inventories may not always have been worn so that they showed. Other court fashions such as the *houppelande* were also adopted somewhat late: at the close of the fourteenth century in Dijon *houppelandes* and large numbers of hoods are to be found in both masculine and feminine inventories. As far as colour is concerned, black silk is of course absent. Only a few prominent men, with considerable private incomes, wore scarlet as either a gown or a *houppelande*; rich merchants used it only for hoods. In this wealthy but limited urban society it appears that women's wardrobes contained fewer coloured garments and much less expensive fur than men's: squirrel fur was the lining used in several women's best dresses. Coloured fabrics and furs were in regular use, however, by women of all classes, modest townswomen and even peasants. This was probably due to their lifestyle and activities rather than to a more developed interest in dress.

As fashion spread to the less well-to-do (and much more numerous) classes, change in the styles and types of clothing, and in fabrics and colours, began to slow down. Fashions also underwent simplification and modifications that changed their nature to a certain extent. If the iconography is to be believed, the peasant did not go about his business in doublet and hose until the middle of the fifteenth century, whereas artisans are portrayed wearing the same garb from the beginning of the century. Ill-fitting, often shapeless and worn, the clothes depicted have only a distant relationship to the elegant attire worn at

31   Pietro de Crescenzi: *Livre des profits champêtres*. Bibliothèque de l'Arsenal, Paris, MS 5064, f.68, illuminated in Bruges by the Master of Margaret of York in the third quarter of the fifteenth century. According to documents such as this one, labourers, including these grape pickers, wore doublet and hose from the mid-fifteenth century onwards.

court. These images, obviously reflecting reality, show men at work with their hose rolled to the knee or hanging down behind, revealing a pair of underpants or a shirt-tail; they emphasise the importance of the manner of wearing a garment as a contribution to an overall look.

Fashions in accessories spread so rapidly that by the end of the Middle Ages mass-production and trade had taken over. Although the sumptuary laws made every effort to control their use, accessories embellished with precious metals or imitations were widespread; witness to this are the metallic remains found on archaeological sites even in small villages. Silk came to the urban populace in the form of belts and purses in the fifteenth century; trimmed with silver, these figure among the possessions of artisans and wine growers, and also in pawn-brokers' inventories, which suggests that such finery may have represented a way of setting money aside as savings.

The names of colours mentioned in contemporary documents give only a rough idea of the variety of shades used in dress, and an even rougher one of their brightness or depth of colour. They confirm, however, that coloured fabrics were used in all social milieux in the fifteenth century, even if coarse (and often undyed) fabrics were still abundantly used by the lower classes, particularly in the country. Because of the high price of silk, townsfolk were unable to emulate the courtiers, but they had their own fashions. The Dijon archives reveal that between the end of the fourteenth and the end of the fifteenth centuries blue, the most popular colour for years, often accompanied by red and sometimes green, was superseded in popularity by violet for several decades; in the end both were abandoned in favour of black wool. In order to confirm these trends and to identify regional variations it would be useful to have to hand further studies based on documents similar to the ones surviving in Dijon. Illuminated manuscripts and paintings often show only the ruling classes and give a very approximate view of the sartorial customs of society as a whole. They are, on the other hand, an indispensible guide to the manifold varieties of fashions that existed across the whole of the West at the time.

THE GEOGRAPHY OF STYLES

A vast area around the Mediterranean is characterised by its access to the brilliant civilisation of the Byzantine and Islamic worlds, both at a much higher level of economic development than the West in the early Middle Ages. Climate and the types of fabric available certainly played a decisive role in the choice of raw materials and of styles. It is a recognised fact that the fashion for wearing doublet and hose without a tunic was started in Naples by Aragonese soldiers. In the same way the female décolleté was adopted sooner and more rapidly in Italy than further north. Peasants, like their aristocratic counterparts, adapted to the Mediterranean summer heat by wearing more linen clothes, lined with soft fabrics; peasantry and nobility alike wore clothes with front or side openings. At the end of the fourteenth century and throughout the fifteenth the Italians were the first to introduce loose overgarments, open right down the sides and sometimes in front as well, later to be imitated in other parts of the West; one of these was sleeveless (the *huque*) and the other had short, winged

32   Giovanni da Milano: *Birth of the Virgin
Mary* (detail). Rinuccini Chapel, Santa Croce,
Florence, *c.*1365. In Italy dresses had close-
fitting bodices and tight sleeves, flared from
the bust to the floor. Here, on the figure on
the left, the wide necklines and sleeves are
emphasised by a band of gold braid, and a
broad band of coloured fabric from neck to
hem contrasts with the white of the dress.

sleeves (the *journade*). From the mid-fifteenth century fitted clothes
showed off the fine undergarments beneath them. The male doublet
displayed a large triangle of gathered shirt under its front lacing; later
the sleeves of women's gowns, slit and joined at intervals, allowed the
sleeves of the delicate shift (also visible at the neckline) to puff out.

Spain, being geographically off-centre, retained marked individu-
ality in its textiles and in the styling of some of its clothes. The Islamic
influence remained strong until the end of the Reconquest, and in
addition it is difficult to disentangle the contribution made by the
Visigoths from Spain's own contribution. In the tenth century a very
unusual mantle was introduced which opened on the right shoulder
(as did mantles everywhere) but which had a slit on the left side for
the left arm to pass through. In the twelfth and thirteenth centuries
some soldiers wore tunics with skirts consisting of long, mobile bands
made of the same material as the top part; striped fabrics seem to have
been the favourites for these. Slashes and openings on the sides char-
acterise thirteenth-century fashion. For both men and women the
sleeveless surcoat with wide armholes allowed the *cotte* to show, and
the side lacing of the *cotte* in turn allowed a glimpse of the undergarment. A sleeveless overdress setting off the striped sleeves of the

33   Alfonso X the Wise: *Cantigas de Santa Maria*. Real Biblioteca de San Lorenzo, Escorial, T.I. 1, f.150, illuminated in Spain in the thirteenth century. Spanish women wore high headdresses, rising to a point at the back and secured by a chin strap.

undershirt is typical of lower-class women's costume at the end of the fifteenth century. During the fourteenth and fifteenth centuries male fashion seems to have been in line with that of the rest of Europe, while women's clothes developed along more individual lines. The *mantonet*, sometimes shaped like a short cape and sometimes like a straight, waist-length jerkin, was found only in Spain. The same could also be said of the custom (introduced about 1470) of stitching padded hoops to skirts to give them a slight bell-shape. This invention was the origin of the *vertugadin* or farthingale (a hooped underskirt), worn by all ladies of quality in the following century.

In northern and eastern Europe documents and pictures relating to clothing are comparatively scarce and later than those that survive elsewhere. The cut of the clothes worn in the fourteenth century by members of the small Danish colony in Greenland confirms the ubiq-uity of the European model: a full-skirted, thigh-length tunic with a

34   Alfonso de La
Torre: *Delectable
Vision*. Bibliothèque
Nationale, Paris, Esp.
39, f.10, illuminated in
Barcelona in 1477.
Woman wearing a
dress 'à vertugadin'
(i.e., with hoops added
to the outside of the
underskirt) with
detachable sleeves.

hood with a long point. In Poland the rigour of the winters probably
explains the unusual occurrence of cloaks for women; their shape,
gathered round the neck, was also unusual. A statue, dating from
about 1400, shows fine, soft gathers that suggest the use of a textile
rather than leather. The heavier pleats and figured pattern on a late
fifteenth-century mantle almost certainly indicate the use of small
animal skins, stitched together to make a garment to be worn with
the fur outermost. The adoption of the caftan in Hungary and Poland
is difficult to date exactly. Although representations of rulers in
majesty and armed warriors predominate until the fifteenth century,
there are more everyday images that depict male figures wearing long,
straight garments, lined, with buttons right down the front, which are
undoubtedly connected with the oriental tradition. In the central
landmass of Europe it is not so easy to identify regional variants. The
network of influences, particularly in the early medieval period when
images are still few and far between, is difficult to disentangle.

From the thirteenth century onwards, sculpture, illuminated manuscripts and painting reveal generalised differences which focus
largely on the ornamentation of clothing and headgear. In Spain the

35 *The Ten Commandments* (detail). National Museum, Warsaw, painted in Gdansk *c*.1480. Polish ladies wore long capes gathered at the neck, sometimes made of fur, with the fur on the outside. Their tall headdresses draped with white linen earned them the nickname 'white ladies'.

cylindrical caps and coifs took an unusual turn in the second half of the thirteenth century. The cap found in the tomb of the Infante Fernando de la Cerda, made of cloth of gold embossed with the royal coat of arms and decorated with bands of gilded leather and gold is

36   *King Wenceslas Bible*. University Library, Prague, MS XXIII, C 124, f.72, illuminated in Bohemia *c*.1340. This young lady's veil is bordered with several rows of ruching.

similar in appearance to the caps depicted in the illuminated manuscripts of the period. Women's headdresses were similar in general outline, but were held in place by a chin strap and were even taller; they were cylindrical in shape with the addition occasionally of a vertical point at the back.

The Germanic lands and their neighbours, from the fourteenth century on, had definite preferences in the adornment of their clothing, although it is difficult to know where these originated. Dagged edges in the shape of crenellations, triangles and leaves (round or lobed), used to edge clothing, enjoyed a great vogue in the second half of the fourteenth century, and their use by both men and women continued in the fifteenth century. Hoods, mantles and wide sleeves were decorated with these daggings. Frills and fluted fabric were reserved for women's clothing, sometimes adorning long, loose sleeves, but mainly being used for women's headdresses. From

37   Pisanello: *Study of the Head of a Woman*. Department of Drawings, Louvre, Paris, first half of the fifteenth century. The women of northern Italy wore an almost spherical *balzo* on the back of their heads.

Bohemia to Scandinavia, and from Flanders to England, the fine veils preferred by ladies of the nobility to horned headgear or the pointed *hennin*, were edged with frills, sometimes several layers of them.

Italian women's preference for light headdresses, consisting of plain headbands or transparent veils, was occasionally eclipsed. In the mid-fourteenth century, for example, well-dressed women began to wear large hats with a beaked brim, a style made fashionable by men. About 1430 a very individual headdress was invented in northern Italy, the *balzo*: this large sphere worn far back on the head was constructed either from hair and plaited hair held in a net, or from a textile covering. Though smaller, women's headdresses in Poland always provided maximum cover and were quite different from the frilled veils of their Bohemian and German neighbours. In the fourteenth century they consisted of a padded circlet but in the fifteenth century they gained height; they were entirely covered in white veiling which closely enwrapped the head and neck, earning the sobriquet of 'white heads' for the women who wore them.

The varieties of clothing and headgear known from surviving illustrations were the sole province of the well-to-do, almost exclusively the aristocracy and the world of the court. There are too few images, and the information in documents is too cursory to establish details about regional differences in dress and the manner in which women from different villages would express these. Some information on the matter has nevertheless survived.

PART THREE
SIGNS AND SIGNIFIERS

CHAPTER SEVEN

The Cycles of Life

EVERYONE IS NAKED AT BIRTH; medieval man is rarely depicted
with clothes on at his burial. Absence of clothing, however, whether
exceptional or routine, was accepted and represented in the Middle
Ages without either false shame or exhibitionism. The clothed state
was the norm, nevertheless, and a number of factors interacted with
the sumptuary laws to tailor each person's appearance to his social
group and his financial situation. Age and marital status also had bearing on the choice of materials and styles, as well as on interest in
fashion (or its rejection). The sum of these attitudes was expressed in
particular modes of dressing on the occasion of rites of passage such
as birth, marriage or death.

THE NUDE AND THE NAKED

The connotations carried by nudity in medieval society as a whole
were far less negative than they have become in modern times. It
seems to have been accepted practice to undress before going to bed
and to sleep with nothing on, at any rate by those in possession of a
bed and bed linen. A pole fixed horizontally to a wall near the bed
held the clothes worn during the day, including the shirt. Linen was
in short supply at this period and documents make no mention of
nightshirts. The head would be covered at night, either by a nightcap
or a piece of fabric wound round like a turban. At this period it was
only the quantity and texture of the fabric that established any social
distinctions. Pictorial representations are on the whole late, and show
this type of scene taking place in comfortable interiors in which couples have their own room, but this was by no means the case for
everybody. Town dwellers and villagers of moderate means did not
have sufficient space for each inhabitant of a dwelling to have their
own beds where they could sleep naked. Nakedness by then anyway
seems to have been reserved for intimacy between couples, at night.

As soon as the person depicted in bed, in childbirth or ill-health, is integrated into a more inclusive network of social relationships, then clothing (at least a nightshirt) is worn.

For bathing, nudity was also the norm, whether the baths were taken simply for reasons of hygiene or for therapeutic effect. The figures represented (somewhat schematically) taking the waters at Puzzoli are entirely naked. Medicinal baths could also be prepared at home by adding infusions of plants and other substances prepared by an apothecary to the hot water. Illustrations sometimes show baths with what amounts to a canvas tent on top, open to allow access to the bather. The aim of the canvas structure appears to have been less to conceal nudity than to protect the bather from cold and to concentrate the medicinal vapours. Medical theory had not yet come to consider water as bad for the health, and indeed prescribed its use for newborn babies, mothers in labour and for a wide range of illnesses. Bathing was nevertheless seldom undertaken at home. Even the wealthiest urban homes seldom had private bathrooms. Household inventories reveal how very rare bath tubs were in the fifteenth century, except perhaps in the homes of clerics, who would possess a bath because of the ill-repute surrounding public bath houses, rather than for reasons of modesty.

Bathing establishments were common in towns, and the authorities would try to ensure that men and women did not use them together. Nakedness was customary for bathers, and the attendants wore only very light shifts. Well-cooked meals with plentiful wine were often served to people in the bath tub itself. The transformation of public bath houses into dens of vice and prostitution, progressively closed or abandoned by a populace without the wherewithal to practise hydrotherapy at home, probably helped to break the custom of social nudity whose roots were to be found deep in Antiquity.

Outside the towns some seigneurial families had systems for baths and bathing in their castles. Although denied this luxury, their servants and the local peasantry, rich or poor, did not have to do without the pleasure of water completely. Solitary or all-male baths are frequently represented. The documents in which they occur show that they were everyday occurrences, taken from reality: for example, a falconer swims across a small lake with all his clothes (apart from his cap) piled in a heap on the bank; harvesters, also stark naked, swim in a river or dry themselves in the sun. Women on the other hand hardly ever appear except in set pieces – illustrations to the Bible, for

38   *King Wenceslas Bible.* Österreichische Nationalbibliothek, Vienna, MS. 2759, f.174v, illuminated in Bohemia *c*.1389–1400. The person being washed is completely naked, while the two servants are wearing very light shifts and wear nets on their hair.

example, such as Bathsheba's bath, or mythological scenes such as bathing in the fountain of Youth – which suggests that female nudity was a much less frequent or socially acceptable phenomenon than its male counterpart.

Partial nudity was also more freely practised by men than by women, in the open air as well as at home. The many images of agricultural labour in summer show peasants making hay or cutting corn wearing only a shirt; sometimes *braies* extend below the shirt, more frequently short underpants can be glimpsed through the opening of the shirt. In Mediterranean areas where the grape harvest takes place in the full heat of summer, grape pickers and barrel hoopers work in the same kind of clothes. Many other professions, some dirty, some carried out near sources of heat, involve complete or partial undress: potters, charcoal burners, metalworkers were often as lightly clad as harvesters. Once two-piece clothing had been adopted the doublet was frequently worn open or partially undone and the hose, held up by aglets in front, were rolled to below the knee.

Women appear to have been much more reticent about baring their bodies. In later representations of agricultural labour in which men and women are shown working side by side, the women cutting corn, stooking, haymaking and picking grapes show a certain reserve. They exchange their long-sleeved, high-necked dresses for low-necked *cotte*, open in front, with short sleeves under which the long sleeves of the undershirt extend. At most they tuck the front of the *cotte* up into their belt, revealing an undershirt of the same length as the *cotte*, buttoned up the front and very full. The few references to women's *braies* must be taken for what they were – very exceptional. At home the lady of the house could also be identified by her *cotte* as she went about her household chores. The overdress would be put on only to go out or for warmth. Representations of humble dwellings, showing the way the members of the household dressed when at home, are scarce. It seems likely that men enjoyed the same freedom to undress at home as they did in the workshop or in the fields; if some of the courtly romances are to be believed, soldiers felt no embarrassment about going into ladies' chambers in their under-shirts 'to have themselves scratched'.

Erotic references to nakedness or semi-nakedness are not of course completely absent from medieval literature. Writers, like painters, were inspired by female nudity; feminine seduction is often symbol-ised by the siren, a woman in the upper part of her body, with her long hair spread over her shoulders, and a bird or animal below. It is the hair, in fact, rather than the nudity that would subsequently char-acterise temptresses and seductresses; Salome and the Great Whore of Babylon are women elegantly and expensively dressed, in the latest fashion, often portrayed combing their hair in front of a mirror. It was the rediscovery of antique sculpture in Italy in the fifteenth century that brought about the proliferation of images of the nude. Not all modes of artistic expression achieved the austere sobriety of Antiquity at once, and for a long time temptresses based on Classical history and mythology adorned their frail forms with the jewels, hats and other headdresses then in favour with ladies of noble birth.

In contrast to this slightly ambiguous (but generally valued) view of nakedness, and to the innocent nudity of every day, was the state of undress inflicted as insult or punishment. To knock the hat off a man's head, to pull the headdress off a woman or to attack her cloth-ing, constituted breaches of personal dignity that had to be settled in court. The vanquished soldier, prisoner of the enemy, had to aban-don his armour and most of his clothing. To add to the shame of sur-render, townsfolk sometimes had to undergo the further humiliation of kneeling before their conqueror in their shirt-sleeves and handing him the keys to their city. Prisoners condemned to capital punish-ment were led to their deaths wearing only a shirt. In the fifteenth century those led to the pillory still wore only a shirt and a crown of straw; at least the custom of promenading adulterous couples through the streets on horseback (or on a donkey), naked or in shifts, seems by then to have died out. The wording of lighter sentences emphasises the symbolic value (in law) of certain items of clothing. Even important people sometimes had to make amends for crimes they had committed bare-headed and without a belt. To demonstrate her renunciation of any claim on her husband's inheritance, a widow would remove her belt and place it on the deceased man's grave.

THE AGES OF LIFE

The idea that, in order to flourish and grow, a child, born naturally good, should be unconstricted by his clothing, is far removed from medieval notions of childcare. On the contrary, the child's frailty needed protection, all parts of the body were to be kept straight, rectified, a sense of shaping that had moral implications as well. From the thirteenth century onwards, artists produced increasing numbers of pictures of children from the moment of birth. The nakedness of the baby receiving its first bath symbolised the destitution of mankind coming into the world deprived of any symbols of status as well as a first purification by water, prefiguring that of baptism. The clothing babies received at birth had remained unchanged since Classical times, and indeed changed very little before the twentieth century. There was no sewn clothing for the newborn baby. A large square of soft fabric covered the umbilical binding and enveloped the baby completely, covering the head like a kind of hood. Later, the baby was swaddled in a woollen blanket which was folded and fastened in front through two thicknesses. The lower point of the triangle was folded over the feet to protect them. The arms were generally strapped into this bundle and the whole kept in place by broad bands: in Italy, and particularly in Tuscany, a spiral wrapping technique was preferred; elsewhere looser intertwining of the bands was more common, which not only facilitated changing the baby but gave it more freedom of movement. Contemporary painters and miniaturists accentuate (by the colours they used) the very pronounced differences between the clothing of rich and poor parents. Rich infants wore very white linen, bound with red braid as recommended in medical treatises, reiterating beliefs probably handed down from much earlier times. Poor children had to make do with greyish swaddling clothes made from hempen fabric, and drab coloured bindings.

Once the child reached a few months, in summer (or weather permitting), its shoulders and arms were released, or clothed in a fitted

39   *Saint Dorothy* (detail). Department of Prints, Bibliothèque Nationale, Paris, engraving executed in Swabia in the fifteenth century. Jesus, looking like any young child of the day, wears only a red linen shirt, open down the front.

vest. The swaddling clothes continued to be worn below the armpits. The head was occasionally protected by a bonnet of great luxury for royal babies, by a cotton bonnet or knitted cap for all others. In certain areas bandages or tight bonnets continued the cranial manipulation begun by the midwife to elongate the head.

At the next stage, when the child was learning to walk, a padded roll (*bourrelet*) would be tied on its head to protect it. The wearing of swaddling clothes ceased and the child would be dressed in a loose dress, long, wide and often split down the sides, worn without undergarments. Although images tend to portray children with bare feet, shoe-sellers' stocks suggest that socks and shoes were in general use. At this stage clothing was the same for either sex; the gowns grew gradually shorter and more like the gowns worn by adults, soon beginning to reflect the economic status of the parents. Just before a child reached the age of seven the clothes began to be differentiated: boys received tunics and doublets similar to those worn by grown men, girls long, fitted gowns. Unlike adults, children wore nothing on their heads; girls wore their hair loose on their shoulders. At seven years old the sons of the nobility began their apprenticeship with weapons and received their first armour. Throughout childhood the choice of

40 Jean Bouteiller: *La Somme rurale*. Bibliothèque Nationale, Paris, Fr. 202, f.15v, illuminated by Loyset Liédet in 1471. Tree of life showing changes in the costume of an aristocratic woman at different ages.

colours for clothing was guided by belief in their symbolic associations. The brightest colours, red and green in particular, were available to only the most fortunate; others had to make do with clothes of dull brown or faded blue, often made from their parents' cast-offs.

Entry into active life and the legal age of majority coincided with the start of adolescence; this was also when the age of seduction began, when the young, unmarried man would avail himself of all the finery he could lay hands on. Images of the different ages of man lay special emphasis on adolescence. Late medieval miniatures attribute to this stage of life the most fashionable clothing and the brightest colours, with a preference for green, the colour of spring. The young man may wear a big hat or a tall cap, in imitation of the courtiers, and he wears a dagger hanging from his belt.

41   *Heures de Rohan*. Bibliothèque Nationale, Paris,
Lat. 9471, f.33v, illuminated by the Master of Rohan
in Anjou *c*.1419–27. The Virgin Mary, nursing her
child, wears a dress laced across the bust.

Young women and girls, of only marginal importance, hardly ever appear in these images. Even pictures of court life accord them only a minor role, and women are often portrayed in more stereotyped fashion than men. For women, youth was primarily the age of fertility. Whether the theme is sacred or profane, pregnancy, childbirth and breastfeeding epitomise the principal function of women, maternity. From the shift to the gown, women's clothes were cut very generously, the surcoat being split down both sides to accommodate pregnancy. The front of the *cotte* was fastened by an adjustable lacing which allowed the garment to adapt to changes of shape, as did the belt, tied high under the bust or around the hips. The colours were youthful, green, red and bright blue, to emphasise the fullness of life of the young mother suckling her baby, be it through the front of her *cotte*, through specially enlarged side seams or through armholes cut very low. Soon, however, came the age of *chaperons* and coifs, of high-necked dresses, the renunciation of bright colours and the adoption of dark shades.

In representations of the ages of man, the adult male abandoned green when tight-fitting clothes became less fashionable. Royal account books are among the few contemporary documents from which the ages of the people listed can be estimated, and they confirm that it was young people (first men, later women) who spent the most money on dress and were the first to adopt fashionable colours, new styles and modish furs. This marked a strong move away from the generally conservative styles maintained by their superiors. In court circles green was reserved for adolescents and younger children, being worn only on exceptional occasions by the young men and women – for Maytime celebrations, for instance. As girls or young married women, princesses seem to have had a particular liking for silks and metallic fabrics in blue. The red of crimson silk or scarlet wool, on the other hand, was worn by people of all ages. Ageing does not seem to have had any particular influence on the type of clothing ordered by a prince, nor on his manner of dressing. Even as a septuagenarian, René d'Anjou continued to have the same type of clothes made for him: doublets, jerkins, short gowns. There is no reason to suppose that he muffled himself in the long gowns and huge overcoats in which miniaturists rig out their old men. The number of mantles he ordered was no greater when he was older than it had been when he was a young man, and his consumption of furs was less.

42   Valerius Maximus: *Histoire des Gracques*. Bibliothèque Nationale, Paris, Fr.
20320, f.307, fifteenth century. Long robes and very full cloaks were, for
medieval artists, the distinguishing features of old people.

RITES OF PASSAGE

From the cradle to the grave, the great landmarks of human existence
have always been marked by ceremonies that gather family and
friends around the person involved. Birth is generally regarded as
sacred in all religions, and along with the founding of a new family
and departure from life was marked in medieval Christianity by rituals
of special solemnity. Religious minorities, more tolerated than
accepted and sometimes rejected, conducted festivals of a more inti-
mate nature. Rites of passage connected with professional life also
existed, including acceptance into a trade or a guild, but little is
known about such ceremonies compared with those celebrating the
admittance of a soldier to the status of knight, or the accession of a
prince to a royal or imperial throne, ceremonies strongly associated
with the Church. These promotions to the higher echelons of the
honours system were symbolised by the individual's donning special
clothes. Similarly, on entering a monastic order, particular habits
were adopted. The rituals of such transitions can only be analysed if
the meanings associated with the clothing is borne in mind.

Holy baptism, the rite celebrating entry into the Christian life, was celebrated in different ways for infants from different backgrounds. In the early days of Christianity baptism was administered (to adolescents and young adults) by total immersion in a pool of water, with the neophyte virtually naked. From the Carolingian period onwards, the Church and theologians had to struggle to get new-born babies baptised. Probably in acknowledgment of the frailty of the average baby, priests began to pour the baptismal water only over the forehead; the baby was still presented virtually naked to this washing and oiling with sacred oils, before being wrapped in its swaddling clothes again. The fine linen cloth then wound around the baby to envelop it completely symbolised the spotless purity of the new Christian, cleansed of original sin. The infant's baptismal veil or 'chrismal' figures in a number of inventories. It must have been marked or embroidered in some way to distinguish it from the other pieces of fine linen in the chest, and would probably have been lent out to families not possessing one. This was the only ritual garment associated with baptism. Among the rich and powerful, the ceremony came to be conducted with ever-increasing extravagance: the infant might be wrapped in a fur-lined blanket slightly resembling a lined hood (almuce); in the fifteenth century royal children were carried to the baptismal font wearing velvet mantles embellished with ermine and trains that were sometimes several metres long. Neither the godparents nor any other member of the congregation wore any special distinguishing garment or sign. The infant's real parents would be absent; according to some accounts, the father refrained from attending and the mother was still resting after her confinement. On the way back from church the godmother would bring the baby wrapped in its baptismal veil to the mother's chamber.

Marriage, at first simply a civil contract, was progressively taken over by the Church until it was promoted to become a sacrament. Representations of royal marriages are numerous in late medieval iconography; the couple are seen exchanging vows at the foot of the altar, generally in the presence of a bishop with cope and mitre. By this time the custom of holding a pall of exquisite fabric over the married couple seems to have been abandoned in princely circles, though illustrations show it still in use among the less exalted. The length of coloured cloth is held high above the heads of the couple, who are seen kneeling before the priest at the entrance to the church. Among written accounts of this custom there is one, dating from the end of the fourteenth century, that tells of a noble lord buying a length of

43   Boccaccio: *Teseida*. Österreichische Nationalbibliothek, Vienna, MS 2617, f.182, illuminated by Colin d'Anjou *c*.1470. The marriage of Emilia and Palemon; the type of clothing worn at this ceremony depends on the age and dignity of the wearers.

green damask to be held above him at the celebration of his nuptial mass.

There were no traditional clothes for the married couple; each, according to his rank and fortune, wore the best that he had. Royal couples probably wore one of the sumptuous outfits from their trousseau. From the early fourteenth century onwards, queens and princesses gave a silken gown and mantle to noble members of their entourage who were getting married, although these were people who would normally have worn only wool. Public records from the thirteenth century onwards reveal that wedding clothes form part of the property that a father has to provide for his daughters; numerous documents instance good quality woollen cloth bought by rich peasants for their daughters' wedding dress. When dictating their last will and testament, fathers of daughters of marriageable age bequeath sums of money for the purchase of the fabrics that are needed in order to put up a good show on their wedding day, and also for the purchase of a jewelled (sometimes imitation) chaplet or garland to wear on their head.

The finery specifically associated with marriage was mainly jewellery. Belts, and to an even greater extent rings and brooches, often bear emblems or inscriptions taken from the repertoire of lovers, and some were identifiable enough for the person drawing up an inventory to note, among other jewellery, a 'bridal clasp'. The exchange of wedding rings, so often featured in contemporary illustrations, is confirmed by archaeological finds; even in the simplest rustic homes, plain bronze or copper rings were kept with the household treasures. The bride wore no special outfit; veils were worn for many different occasions and do not seem typical. As a general rule the engaged couple did not wear any particular colour, although in some Mediterranean areas there was a predilection for red. In inventories of women's clothing farther north, red does not figure very largely; it can be deduced that young village women wore a blue wedding dress, often accompanied by a red *chaperon*, of the kind mentioned in their posthumous inventories. The celebrations arranged for princely weddings engendered a tremendous display of elegance and extravagance, for the religious ceremony as well as for the tournaments and jousting that regularly followed encounters between rival courts. No apparent signs or special signals singled out the married couple or the members of their cortège. In some of the miniatures or paintings, various people are wearing coronets of flowers, a frequent ornament for the head at this period; these probably symbolise the festive atmosphere rather than the solemnisation of marriage.

Customs for Jewish marriages varied over the centuries and in different parts of the diaspora. The bridegroom would wear the outfit he usually wore to the synagogue to pray; over his shoulders he would drape a rectangular piece of cloth with fringes at the corners, the *tallit*. Occasionally, he would also wear a full-length overgarment of white linen. A garment of this type was worn by the bride at a marriage in the Rhineland in the fifteenth century. She also wore a garland or coronet on her head and a veil that had to be long enough to cover her eyes. During the ceremony, a *tallit* was held over the heads of the couple, in the same way as the pall was held over Christian couples.

The rituals accompanying the exit from life imposed stricter dress codes. The Church had struggled to put an end to pagan customs relating to death since the beginnings of Christianity, combating the

44   *Book of Hours.* Bibliothèque Municipale, Dijon, MS 1268, f.126v, illuminated in Paris in the early fourteenth century. In the fourteenth century the
people accompanying a funeral cortège were often dressed in bright colours.

cremation favoured in Antiquity as much as the clothed burial practised by the barbarians. The Church attached the greatest importance
to the soul, assisted in its passage into the next world by two sacraments, penance and extreme unction. The body is only the recepta-
cle of the soul; as such, it must be treated with respect and simplicity,
and be returned to the earth naked, wrapped in a winding sheet of
linen or cotton, which could be tied like a baby's swaddling clothes,
pinned or stitched. There were recognised exemptions from this rule
for monarchs and bishops, who would be interred in abbeys or cathedrals clothed in the vestments of their office.

The use of a pall to cover the coffin during the funeral ceremony
was widespread. Derived from the pallium, which since late
Antiquity had signified both a canopy and a liturgical vestment, it was
first used to accompany the mortal remains of dignitaries. From the
thirteenth century onwards, however, less exalted folk specify in their
wills the quality and colour of cloth with which they wish to be
covered during their obsequies. Townsfolk and simple members of
the clergy, who have never worn such sumptuous fabrics in their lifetime, order the purchase of cloth of gold or silk, marked with a great

cross in a contrasting colour. The intention was not in fact solely to flatter the deceased; in most cases it is stipulated that the pall should be turned into ornaments for the church afterwards, a pious bequest designed to draw the memory of the deceased into divine worship. It was not until the second half of the fourteenth century that funeral palls ceased to be coloured and became black, undoubtedly under the influence of mourning garb.

Although the custom of public lamentation was contrary to Christian notions of death, the Church had not managed to eradicate it; mourners wailed and made gestures, with their clothes in disorder. The habit of wearing black mourning clothes, attributed to the Spanish, was adopted by French and English royalty at the beginning of the fourteenth century; because of the high price of fabrics it spread very slowly. Courtiers and their servants received lengths of black wool of a quality carefully adjusted to their social status and position in the hierarchy. The long, trailing cloaks and huge hoods pulled down over the face, made known through fifteenth-century statuary, were confined to the rich.

This ostentatious form of mourning dress, designed for the funeral cortège, probably did not last very long. There are few surviving records of medieval practice. The Duke of Burgundy, Philip the Good, wore nothing but black after the assassination of his father in 1419; Louis XI, on the other hand, with the approval of his advisers on etiquette, wore red as soon as his father's funeral was over in order to demonstrate the permanence and continuity of royalty. The widowed queens of France wore white veils, wimples and *tourets*, thus earning themselves the name of 'white queens'. Such headdresses, which gave them the appearance of nuns, were not only worn by mourning royalty. The many funeral effigies that survive in England, featuring noble or (less frequently) middle-class women, confirm the stringency of the dress regulations imposed on widows: wimples right up to the chin; veils covering their foreheads and much of their cheeks; faces shaded by capacious hoods. But this was not common practice; for the average person bereavement was seldom, if ever, reflected in clothing.

Chapter Eight

Clothes as Identification Markers

ALL CLOTHING CONVEYS SOMETHING about its wearer, but there are some combinations or single items that transmit a stronger, and yet a more exclusive signal. Positive marks of identification, from the rich ornamentation of the highest ranks to the simplest aids to recognition, have been employed throughout history. Negative markers on clothing, on the other hand, are not always so straightforward. They may be adopted as a deliberate way of dissociating oneself from society and its values, temporarily or permanently. In the Middle Ages, various members of society were forced to wear visible signs of exclusion or infamy, strong evidence of the importance attached to clothing as identification of its wearer.

THE OUTWARD EXPRESSION OF DIGNITY

Christian ecclesiastical costume does not aim to glorify the celebrant in person, but rather his role as Christ's representative during the commemoration of the Last Supper. Church vestments did not become extravagant until about the sixth century. The early Church advised priests to celebrate mass in their ordinary clothes, the clothes of the romanised West, to which a few regional variations were added. When the clothing worn by the barbarian tribes began to prevail, the Church rejected it, prescribing a type of clothing to be worn for religious services that was distinct from the clothing in general use. From the Carolingian period onwards painters frequently depicted ecclesiastical figures – saints or contemporary characters – but they evidently took their inspiration from the clerical dress worn by bishops or imperial chaplains. Outside the Church all covered their clothes with an alb, a generously cut tunic of white cloth with long sleeves, tied round the waist with a cord. Even by this time, however, other items of ecclesiastical dress were made from rich fabrics. With the great abbey at Cluny as a model, churches and royal chapels aimed to surround divine worship with splendour and procured precious silks to enhance their ceremonial.

Although it subsequently went through minor alterations, ecclesiastical dress was established in broad outline from the Carolingian period onwards. To start with, the chasuble was a large circular cloak with a hole in the centre for the head. The dalmatic, a tunic with sleeves, was nearly always decorated in the ancient style with vertical bands over the shoulders and decorative medallions. The cope or 'pluvial' was derived from another type of long mantle worn in Classical times. It opened down the front and originally had a hood which was replaced towards the end of the Middle Ages by an embroidered panel on the shoulders. The cope was initially worn for outdoor ceremonies, but later became the ceremonial mantle. Vestigial forms of other vestments inherited from the Roman world, the maniple and stole, were worn with the chasuble and dalmatic. The maniple was a band of fabric, originally held in the hand, later fixed to the wrist; the stole, worn round the neck under the chasuble, was a long, straight scarf that hung down to the ankles in front. The pallium was at first a long, full mantle but later shrank to the size of a straight band of material worn round the shoulders with long panels hanging down in front and behind; unlike the stole this was worn over the chasuble. The combination of these elements was not yet strictly laid down in order of rank, but bishops were already beginning to wear a mitre in the shape of a hemispherical cap.

The development of liturgical finery is easier to follow after the twelfth century; until the fifteenth century the names of garments remained the same and their shape changed very little. Large churches had substantial incomes and received generous gifts, and were in a position to purchase extravagant silks and to embellish them even further. Until the fourteenth century liturgical vestments were more opulent than princely clothing. Clothing still surviving in church treasuries gives an idea of the high quality of the materials used (mainly cloth of gold and silk), and also of the decorations applied, including the embroidery known as *opus anglicanum*, which entirely covers the fabric of some of the chasubles; the silken threads were gradually enriched with gold and silver thread, with pearls and even with jewellery. The earliest known examples in the West of such techniques as 'knotless netting' and knitting with four or five needles are evident in items like ecclesiastical gloves.

The classification of ecclesiastical garments within the hierarchy was probably initially based on the quality of the fabrics and their ornamentation; once the rules governing the combination of clothing had been established the grading became much clearer. Episcopal pomp was expressed by a dalmatic worn over the chasuble; a priest would wear only a chasuble and a deacon a dalmatic, which now changed its shape, becoming straighter and shorter, with side splits, short sleeves and two ornamental vertical bands, the last vestiges of the primitive tunic on which it was based. The few new additions were introduced in the eleventh to twelfth centuries: the amice was wrapped round the neck and formed a collar under the chasuble; hose and sandals joined the episcopal mitre, crosier and gloves as symbols of the bishop's supreme eminence. The mitre took on a new shape, the original white-linen, hemispherical cap becoming more elongated in the eleventh century and developing points or horn-like protuberances on either side, created by a dent in the centre running from front to back. In the thirteenth century, this was turned round the other way, forming a tall, divided hat and giving the roughly triangular shape that has continued to be used to the present day. In the medieval period mitres were covered with pearls and embroidery, sometimes with jewels and jewellery as well, and were sold in jeweller's shops. The shape of the papal tiara was adopted definitively in the first half of the fourteenth century; originally it was only a small cap worn between ceremonies at which the mitre was the official headdress. The gold border was superseded by a coronet in the twelfth century, then the height of the crown was increased by the addition of a second coronet at the end of the thirteenth century and a third in 1334, endorsing the triple sovereignty of the Pope, spiritual, temporal and judicial.

The decoration of the textiles used for making ecclesiastical vestments generally had no connection with their intended use. The surviving garments or those described in medieval inventories often bear pagan designs inherited by Byzantine workshops from Sassanian silk fabrics. There are later examples of Islamic striped fabrics woven with Arabic inscriptions known to have been used for religious ceremonies. Added decorative elements such as medallions or embroidered gold bands or, later, paintings, generally take their theme from the Bible or from the life of Christ and the saints, or from Christian symbolism.

The symbolism of colours also began to influence the liturgy. By

45 *Vie et miracles de Saint Amand*. Bibliothèque Municipale, Valenciennes, MS 501, f.58v, illuminated in Saint-Amand after 1150. The missionary bishop Saint Amand, shown here with Saint Baudremon, is wearing a dalmatic and chasuble over his alb. At this period the mitre was just a hemispherical cap.

46 Piero della Francesca: *Saint Augustine*.
Museu de Arte Antiga, Lisbon, 1459–69. The
cope has a broad border of orphreys depicting
historical scenes. The mitre is also decorated with
orphreys and precious stones.

the late Middle Ages the meaning of colour had been codified, but differed from bishopric to bishopric. The big festivals were celebrated in red and white, red symbolising the blood of Christ and, by analogy, the blood of the martyrs, brilliant white symbolising light and divinity. While aristocratic society might pass the time by working out the relationship between colours and the stages of a love affair, the Church established a relationship between colours and the theological and cardinal virtues or the manifestations of godliness. Bearing in mind the range of colours established after the Middle Ages, it is interesting to note that purple in the early period possessed none of the connotations of sadness and repentance that it was to acquire later, when its use was restricted to Lent and Advent. In the fourteenth century these periods in the liturgical calendar were expressed (in royal chapels) by the use of white vestments made of plain coloured silk and decorated with simple designs in black ink. The use of black in the fifteenth century appears to have been a reflection of fashions in clothing rather than of any idea of mourning or sadness, and the extravagant decorations and lining in bright colours endorse this hypothesis. Blue, which later disappeared from the liturgical colour scheme, was still in use at this period. It is not surprising that lay tastes should have been influential in Church matters. One principal source of supply of liturgical garments was the generosity of the congregation: princely ledgers and wills provide ample evidence of this. Gifts might be in the form of new fabrics by the yard, to be used by the Church as it pleased or, alternatively, ornaments commissioned by a prince and covered with his coat of arms or decorations of his choosing. Sometimes the gift would be a worn silk garment, bequeathed to the Church to be cut down and made into a liturgical vestment.

The chasuble and its accessories were worn only for the celebration of the mass. For many religious occasions, especially in church, a long, fine linen tunic, the surplice, worn over ordinary clothes, was the accepted attire. This was not strictly speaking a liturgical garment, however, and it was not worn only by priests: deacons, curates and choirboys wore it over a long gown. In the normal course of life, for visiting the sick or bringing them the sacraments, the consecrated cleric would have only one distinguishing feature, very pronounced tonsure. No special mode of dress was required. The synod enjoined the clergy to be moderate: expensive fabrics and furs were forbidden, as were certain colours and the short costume of the fourteenth and fifteenth centuries. The civil clothing of members of the clergy,

47   Justinian: *Infortiatum*. Biblioteca Malatestiana, Cesena, MS S.iv.2, f.111, illuminated in Bologna in the fourteenth century. The priest is giving communion to a dying man; he is wearing a simple blue cloak with a hood.

however, bears no resemblance to the splendid liturgical vestments in use in church; until the closing years of the Middle Ages it bore no indication of rank whatsoever. A bishop could not be identified by colour or by any other feature. In 1245 cardinals, on the other hand, won from the Pope the privilege of wearing a wide-brimmed red hat encircled with silken cords that hung down behind; this was often worn over a bonnet or cap and, from the end of the thirteenth century on, was worn over an item of clothing reserved for cardinals, the *cappa*, a huge circular cloak with a large, fur-lined hood. Scarlet was at the time reserved for papal envoys; it was not adopted by the Sacred College until the end of the fifteenth century when it became the outward symbol of the superiority and dignity of the princes of the Church. Neither purple nor silk was worn at this period; the inventories of certain prelates mention only scarlet, a woollen cloth of the finest quality and, if contemporary images are to be believed, vivid red in colour.

The Church of Rome Triumphant set itself high above royalty in the social hierarchy; considering itself to be the sole possessor of revealed truth, it had little interest in other faiths. The Jewish minorities of the Western diaspora, alternately tolerated and persecuted,

48   Iacob Ben Aser: *I quattro ordini*, Biblioteca Apostolica, Vatican, Rossi 555, f.12v, illuminated in Lombardy *c.*1435. Jewish worship: members of the congregation wear the *tallit* with corners decorated with the *ziziyyot*.

continued their religious practices at home or at the synagogue – daily prayers, the Sabbath and the great annual ceremonials. Texts and images are seldom specific in their interpretations of Biblical passages or traditional writings concerning costume related to particular religious practices. The general attitude to dress, based on the Talmud, can be summed up as 'the glory of God is man and the glory of man is his clothing'. Created by God, the Jew must wear clean clothes when he goes to pray, and if possible certain clothes should be reserved for the synagogue and the Sabbath alone. The custom of keeping the head covered during prayer, or at home, is not biblical in origin; men did not always observe it, but women were strictly obliged to veil their heads in all circumstances. On the other hand the regulation about wearing a fringed shawl did have its origin in the Bible, in the Book of Numbers, and was repeated in the prayer that is the cornerstone of Judaism. The fringes, *ziziyyot*, at the four corners of the rectangular mantle called the *tallit*, had to be worn by men, but the tradition got lost with the dispersion of the Jews. When Talmudic learning was resuscitated in the West after the eleventh century, it was renewed but in a slightly different form. The new *tallit*, a piece of white linen or wool, had fringes and was worn only for ritual purposes; it can be identified in illustrations dating from the thirteenth and early fourteenth centuries being worn by the celebrant at religious ceremonies. It is not until the fifteenth century that Italian and German representations show all the assembled congregation wearing the *tallit*. Except when accompanied by the hat worn by a section of the Ashkenazy community, the *tallit* covered the head completely and enveloped the body. The woven stripes near the ends can only be picked out at quite a late date in northern Italy; the wearing of the *tallit* draped over the shoulders like a scarf is documented for the first time in 1471 in a German illustration. At about this time the first indications of luxury crept in, in the shape of embroidery along the edge of the *tallit* worn over the head. The Jewish community showed a certain creativity with their liturgical vestments between the eleventh and fifteenth centuries; uninterrupted observance of the Mosaic law, and the Jews' distance from power, served to keep them aloof from the ceremonials of Christian worship, and also from the pomp and cirumstance of the daily lives of the princes of the Church.

Like the addition of the three crowns to the papal tiara, the adoption of the new cardinals' robes was filled with political overtones. The red vestment with its white fur was intended to express the highest dignity; similar finery was worn by kings for public appearances before the arrival of silk and before advances in fabric dyeing had extended the range of colours. The symbolic meaning of a crown and other emblems of power was undoubtedly stronger than the meaning of clothing. Nevertheless the garments worn by the king at his coronation played an essential role, and they appeared on all the royal seals and in virtually all representations of royalty until the mid-fourteenth century. The royal investiture ceremony took on a religious, quasi-sacramental character in the early Middle Ages; unctions, similar to those used at baptisms and ordinations, were introduced into the ritual of Visigoth Spain, and later into royal ceremonies in England and France. The act of coronation as such began only during the Carolingian period and took place in a religious building, always in the presence of a bishop or a pope. In spite of his dislike for long garments, Charlemagne agreed to wear 'Roman' vestments for his coronation. This doubly prestigious garb (it represented the Roman tradition while bearing great similarity to liturgical vestments) was generally adopted by the rulers of the Western kingdoms in the Middle Ages, and was incorporated into the rituals that were

49 *Gospels of Otto III.* Bayerische Staatsbibliothek, Munich, Clm. 4453, illuminated in Reichenau *c.*1000. Otto III is seen bearing the emblems of his power as Holy Roman Emperor and wearing clothing inspired by that of the Emperors of Byzantium.

beginning to take shape. Like the crown, the mantle handed down from generation to generation symbolised the legitimate descendance of a new king. Until the modern era, the German emperors of the Holy Roman Empire used the opulent coronation cloak of Roger II of Sicily (now in Vienna) and carried the insignia of the Holy Roman Empire, some of them even older than the cloak; inscriptions in Arabic woven into the border of the mantle indicate that it was made in Palermo in 1133. The full-length, semicircular mantle is made of red silk. The embroidery in the centre depicts a palm tree, a symbol of the tree of life; the tree divides the cloak into two halves, each of which is embroidered, symmetrically, with two lions attacking two camels. During the ceremony it was worn over an alb and a dalmatic making an ensemble that was similar to episcopal garb.

The French coronation robes, decorated with the fleurs-de-lis, belong to a later generation, the generation of heraldry. The fleur-de-lis is a solar symbol which had been an emblem of sovereignty since earliest Antiquity; it began to appear on the seal of the kings of France in the twelfth century and assumed a strong religious significance associated with both Christ and the Virgin Mary at the beginning of the thirteenth. From this time onwards the fleur-de-lis also appeared on royal banners. It was probably used earlier on coronation robes than is suggested by documentary evidence which, from the mid-thirteenth century, is primarily concerned with establishing the order of the ceremony. Miniatures illustrating some of the texts make much of the changing of clothes during the course of this rite of passage. On the eve of the coronation the king wore a simple brown robe as a sign of penitence. The following day, standing beside the altar, he removed it and put on some of the royal panoply, including shoes decorated with fleurs-de-lis, before receiving unction. Immediately following this he was robed in a 'jacinth' tunic decorated with fleurs-de-lis and a great matching mantle. The term 'jacinth' refers to a precious stone which can be either blue or red. In the case of the kings of France it was certainly blue, a colour now promoted to the highest dignity, but red was not totally absent; the silk lining of the mantle was red, as were some of the vestments worn underneath. A number of historians have highlighted the importance of the clothes worn for the coronation, and explained their liturgical function and their symbolism.

The coronation ceremony derived its rituals of vigil and donning of appropriate garb from the traditional dubbing ceremony for young knights. Incorporated into a whole religious rite, the proven warrior's entry into an order of chivalry was accompanied by a layman, also a knight, who worked through a series of symbolic actions, including the handing over of the sword and the grand cloak. Not every knight was in a position to act with the same generosity as the kings of the fourteenth century, who gave mantles of scarlet wool to the new knights they wished to honour.

Romances about the Knights of the Round Table remained popular at this time: festivals and tournaments were organised under the patronage of the Round Table, like the ones organised at Windsor by Edward iii in 1344. The reality by no means matched the ideal, as is revealed by the surge of lay orders of chivalry that developed after the second decade of the fourteenth century and which brimmed over into modern times. From Spain to England, and from France to the Holy Roman Empire, the founders were invariably kings or princely rulers. The élite standing of an order could be estimated by the pre-eminence of its founder (and head), by the number of members admitted (usually carefully limited) and also by the hierarchy of members as expressed in clothing, knights and squires being differently attired. The political motive behind these foundations is obvious: by attaching a 'clientèle' of knights to him through an honours system, festivities and spiritual and material benefits, the sovereign could count on support for his military undertakings. With the Reconquest in view, the King of Castile founded his first order in 1325. Edward III, flushed with success in the dynastic quarrel between the House of Valois and the Kings of England, created the Order of the Garter in 1347/8. The choice of blue and gold as his colours, identical to the French coronation cloak, gives a good idea of his intentions. In response, the Ordre de l'Etoile was founded in 1352 by John II, King of France, but this did not last long. A century later Louis XI (without much conviction) founded the royal order of Saint Michael, to compete with the Golden Fleece, which had been established by his rival, Philip the Good, Duke of Burgundy, in 1429. The mantles worn by knights of these two orders, and indeed by most others, were of scarlet wool, but by now the tunics and hoods accompanying them were made of silk also dyed scarlet (the status of woollen cloth dropped drastically during the fifteenth century). When he founded his Order of the Crescent, René d'Anjou stipulated that the mantles of the knights should be of crimson velvet and those of the squires of matching satin; in 1473 Charles the Bold recommended silk velvet for the mantle of the Golden Fleece. This extravagant clothing was worn only at solemn gatherings of the order, known as chapters. Membership was indicated by a chain (bearing symbols of the order) worn round the neck over everyday clothing. Most of the orders disappeared quite soon as the smaller principalities went under. The Order of the Garter in England and the Golden Fleece of the Dukes of Burgundy (who passed it on to the Holy Roman Emperors) owed their survival to the power of the rulers who were at their head.

Like the order of those dedicated to prayer, the clergy, and the order of those dedicated to fighting, the warriors, the third order of society, those dedicated to civilian life, also had its ceremonial costume. The group in control of power in each city (under whatever name they chose to operate) took a pride in their big woollen mantles, usually scarlet and trimmed with fur. Concillors and other parliamentary personnel chose the same style. The universities, founded in the twelfth century, were authorised by the Pope to choose their own costume and they showed a more eclectic taste. The gown worn by graduates at the beginning of their teaching career might be black, mauve or pink and was often striped in many colours. The accompanying hood might be lined with vair or ermine, providing the authorities did not limit the use of fur to doctors of the university. Only the latter were allowed to wear the cap which, in some southern universities, bore a cascade of silk in the colours of the different faculties.

RENUNCIATION

Although religious ceremonies occupied quite an important place in the practices of the orders of chivalry, and although some of the language they used echoed monastic language, their ethos and the clothes they wore were far removed from those of the religious orders. For members of religious orders the renunciation of the world and its vanities was expressed by the wearing of clothing remarkable for its simplicity; membership of a particular community was indicated by uniform clothing. Entrance into the religious life involved a ritual robing. Monks and nuns received clothing to distinguish them from those living in the outside world. The Benedictine rule came into existence in the Mediterranean world; when it was adopted throughout Christendom some concessions had to be made to local conditions, particularly against the cold weather in the more northerly regions. Only a few garments are specific to monastic clothing; both the scapular and cowl are survivals from the late Classical period. As in secular dress, the cowl and scapular were worn over a tunic, and a large cape was thrown over the top in cold weather. Members of the female orders wore more or less the same things, adding a veil that completely covered the head and shoulders; later, wimples and linen bands entirely hid the neck and forehead.

   In the religious upsurge of the eleventh and twelfth centuries, numerous new orders were formed. Their more radical interpretation of the spirit of poverty and simplicity caused them to adopt rules different from the Benedictine ones. The contrast between Benedictine monks, clad in black, and the Carthusians and Cistercians, clad in white or undyed wool, was immediately apparent and soon assumed strong symbolical meaning. The search for austerity sometimes went

50 *La Sainte Abbaye*, British Library, London, Yates Thompson II, f.6v, illuminated in Lorraine *c*.1300. The nuns wear wimples and linen bands, and veils.

further and was conveyed in the use of coarse fabrics, often thread-bare and patched, and by a reduction in the number of garments worn on top of each other; linen and fur were prohibited. Even when the wearing of fur was permitted in cold climates like Germany, some monks imposed intensely austere regimes upon themselves; contrary to what is generally believed, abnegation did not affect personal hygiene and cleanliness, which were laid down in the rule of some orders. Further new orders founded in the thirteenth century were urban in origin and were therefore different in outlook. The Dominicans adopted the white robe and black travel mantle of the pre-existing order, whose rule they had inherited, without seeming to attach too much importance to it. For the Franciscans the ideal of poverty was paramount. Franciscan clothing was glorified in narrative and images of the life of the founder of the order, Saint Francis of Assisi, who broke with his former life by stripping himself of all his clothes and adopting a greyish brown habit. Those orders that stemmed from the Franciscan rule set more store by the poverty of their clothing than did any of the others. This sometimes led to eccentricity in dress, or even repugnant dirtiness. Nicknames descriptive of the friars' dress were used: the Franciscans were known as 'cordeliers' after the thick cord worn as a girdle and distinguished by three knots (representing the vows of poverty, chastity and obedience); the 'sackcloth' friars wore robes of very coarse cloth; the Carmelites brought back from the East (where their order had its origins) a habit with broad stripes which earned them the name 'barred friars'. The disciples of Saint Francis, in particular the Capuchins, preached openly against all forms of extravagance or excess in matters of dress; they even instituted lawsuits agains changes in the colour of the habit, or in the shape of the sandals or hood. Lay dress was viewed with the same degree of intolerance. Their condemnation of female fashions was particularly violent in the fifteenth century, when they claimed to perceive the horns of the Devil in feminine finery. The movement in favour of self-imposed poverty had lay members as well, not all of whom were members of the third order; the simplicity and austerity of their attire gave them an appearance close to that of the religious orders. One invisible way of mortifying the flesh, practised by religious and laymen alike, was the wearing of a hair shirt next to the skin. Contemporary narratives contain numerous references to this, chroniclers even describing beautiful princesses who, in the fifteenth century, wore 'shifts of horsehair' under their silk dresses; the same shifts are to be found listed in the stock records of contemporary mercers.

For purposes of identification the different Benedictine congregations adopted small variations in the cut of their clothing. As new foundations multiplied after the twelfth century, religious attire was differentiated by more than just different interpretations of the vow of poverty. Colour played an important role and was not restricted to variations on black, white and greyish brown. Some of the orders born after the art of dyeing had developed chose a blue or violet scapular or a 'turkey' blue mantle.

The wearing of distinctive insignia on monastic clothing was confined to the military orders and the hospitallers. Their habit was

51 *Codex Manesse*. Universitätsbibliothek, Heidelberg, Cod. Pal. Germ. 848, f.264, illuminated in Zurich *c*.1330. Tannhaüser, the legendary courtly poet, is wearing the black cross and white cloak of the Teutonic knights.

simpler than the monk's habit, consisting of a robe and a mantle in the colour of the order; knights and ordinary sergeants sometimes wore different robes. Grand masters of the orders allowed themselves a little more pomp. In the Templars, for instance, the knights wore white, the sergeants brown and all wore a red cross stitched to their right shoulder. The cross was the most frequently used symbol. The knights hospitallers wore a white Maltese cross on their black habit. The cross of the Teutonic knights was black on a white background. Other orders preferred military insignia: the sword-bearers were so called because of the crossed swords sewn to their mantles. The colours and insignia were repeated on the military attire that accompanied the armour.

Some of the orders, including the Teutonic knights, recruited members on a temporary basis, making them virtually indistinguish-

52 *The Pilgrims at Emmaus* (detail). Germanisches Nationalmuseum, Nuremberg, acquired from the Augustine Friars in Cologne, painted *c.*1460. The hat, with a brim that can be turned down as protection from rain, has a shell and two lead pilgrimage badges pinned to it. The pilgrim's staff is symbolised by a brooch.

able from crusaders setting off on a campaign against the Infidel, or on a pilgrimage to the Holy Land. In the Middle Ages individuals were often named after a visible sign; crusaders were named after the fabric cross which civilians and soldiers stitched to their outer garments when they had made the decision to depart for Muslim lands. Pilgrimages, short and long, were often imposed as penance to expiate a grave misdemeanour; they were widely undertaken and as time went by became a pretext for travel for pleasure. The pious pilgrim went on foot, clothed for his journey in a short, straightish mantle; men wore a hat, women a veil or, later, a hood. Two characteristic accessories accompanied the pilgrim: a long staff and a bag for bread. Pilgrims making their way to Santiago de Compostela soon adopted the habit of stitching a shell from the beach near the sanctuary onto their clothing or their hat. Gradually the custom grew up of making lead or tin badges representing the relic or the saint venerated in other places of pilgrimage. It became very popular in the fourteenth and fifteenth centuries to wear these on the return from a pilgrimage, pinned to the mantle or hat like the scallop shell of St James of Compostela.

SIGNS OF RECOGNITION

Urban archaeology bears abundant witness to the fact that pilgrimage medals or insignia, in the form of amulets or emblems worn by all those who had visited the same holy place, were widely worn from the fourteenth century onwards. Guilds and brotherhoods also had their identifying marks, usually accessories in the case of organisations with a large number of members. As far as clothing was concerned, a coloured hood was sometimes the outward sign of belonging to a particular party; this custom was essentially urban and made its first appearance at uprisings against royal or princely power: in 1379 the people of Ghent in rebellion against the Count of Flanders adopted a white hood as their distinctive uniform.

Identifying marks were most in favour, however, in the world of warriors and rulers. Coats of arms were the first to appear and met with considerable success, probably because the system of identification could be adapted to an individual, a lineage, a fiefdom or an institution simply by juggling a simple set of colours, shapes and figures; although simple, these were full of symbolic significance. Experts agree that recognising an adversary or an ally in combat when, during the eleventh and twelfth centuries, his hauberk and helmet completely covered his head and face. Geometric, animal or floral figures were first painted on the great shields, later being transferred to banners and seals. Coats of arms were gradually codified, the choice of colours and forms being systematised; later they became hereditary.

Coats of arms – painted, engraved, carved, woven – began to appear on all the impedimenta of daily life; their use on clothing, not yet fully researched, seems to have lasted less long and to have been less widespread. Embroidered coats of arms were frequent on the clothing of princes at the end of the thirteenth century and beginning of the fifteenth, mainly on doublets and surcoats worn in battle, jousting and tournaments. Descriptions of jousting (including contemporary pictorial representations) show that the passion for heraldic clothing was waning from the fifteenth century onwards; before long it was confined to the housings worn by horses. The powerful and great, however, male as well as female, were still portrayed on stained glass windows, frescoes and miniature paintings wearing emblazoned clothing. Pictures of the royal coronation in Rheims show the king wearing his mantle covered in fleurs-de-lis, surrounded by vassals sporting floor-length clothing emblazoned with their coats of arms. In miniatures illustrating chronicles of his reign, the sovereign is always portrayed wearing a crown and draped in the royal cloak; it remains unclear whether these images show costume as it was really worn or whether they represent a symbolic way of portraying the great. Confirmation might be had from purchases itemised in the royal and princely account books. In court circles the prince's coat of arms could be worn by subordinates with military functions such as pages, cavalry riders and messengers. All rulers had their herald at arms, a specialist in matters heraldic, who was chosen from these ranks. In the fifteenth century only the herald at arms wore the royal blazon all over his surcoat. Some attendants, in particular messengers, wore an embroidered escutcheon stitched to their clothing, the latter being made from the fabric given them by the king twice a year; illustrations and account books unfortunately do not always reveal whether these escutcheons were coats of arms or 'devices', devices being preferred after the mid-fourteenth century to demonstrate the wearer's allegiance to a powerful man. By this time coats of arms may have been devalued in the eyes of the rich and powerful as a consequence of their success. They were no longer the sole province of the aristocratic warrior class, and increasing numbers of townsfolk and artisans were using them by the end of the Middle Ages; the repertoire of figures was enriched at this period by a collection of objects in everyday use, including items of clothing like gloves, hoods, hose and boots.

The term 'device' was derived from the verb 'to devise', which originally meant 'to imagine' or 'to create'; in the Middle Ages it did not designate simply a word or a phrase used to express a thought or a sentiment, but in heraldry also implied a figure generally laid on a coloured background. The choice of components combining to make a personal emblem was not governed by any rules. Some people changed the arrangement of the objects, or the themes or colours, several times during their lifetime; René d'Anjou, for example, used alternately a tree stump, a filled sail, an orange and a footwarmer. The Duc de Berry, on the other hand, stayed faithful to his double figure of a bear and a swan. In dynastic battles 'devices' took on political significance, as happened with the white rose of the House of York and the red rose of the House of Lancaster, which earned the name of the Wars of the Roses for the struggle for the throne of England. From Charles v onwards, the kings of France chose emblems that were heavily symbolical; the symbols, for example the golden sun, Saint Michael with his sword, the winged white hart, had religious meanings as well as increasing the king's standing, and were passed from generation to generation until the sixteenth century. Changes in background colour indicated crises in the personal or political life of the personage; the general symbolism of the devices is less simple to decipher. The language of colour was rich in meaning but by no means standardised. The few fifteenth-century treatises dealing with the meaning of colours do not give a clear overall picture.

The words and figures of the devices were used by English, French and Italian princes to decorate and mark their manuscripts and their possessions – including even floor tiles. They were appliquéd to the coloured fabrics used for wall hangings and tapestries, and also to standards and pennants. In the fourteenth century the word or figure of the device might appear on the clothing of prominent persons, without necessarily being accompanied by the original colour of the device. It became customary at this time to clothe members of the entourage, whether civilian or military, in the prince's colours and the term 'livery' began to acquire its present meaning as a result. Until now the livery had simply meant the distribution of clothing or fabric in quantities carefully graded according to rank, from the nobleman to the kitchen boy; this was replaced gradually (in the upper échelons) by gifts of money. By the end of the fifteenth century, gifts in kind were distributed only to those lower down the scale, including those continuing to wear the prince's mixed colours – basically the staff of the stables and pages. From the late fourteenth century onwards the term 'livery' was applied to clothing whose colours were associated with the sovereign's device; at that time liveries generally consisted of clothing in two colours, keenly favoured by the aristocracy at the beginning of the century but later abandoned (along with stripes) to the lower orders. These customs have come to light through the account books, which suggest that there was a discrep-

53 Pierre Choisnet: *Livre des trois âges*. Bibliothèque Nationale, Paris, Smith Lesouëf 70, f.18. The grooms wear livery identical with that worn by soldiers in the late fifteenth century.

ancy between the colours of the devices and those of the liveries; in the same distribution, valets might receive robes in which the colours were combined in a completely different manner, according to what their position was at court. Knights, like princes, would distribute annual liveries to the members of their entourage. Civil institutions began to emulate them; in many towns the municipal authorities would give a gown to their officers, and these gowns might be in two colours or they might have a symbolic figure embroidered on the sleeve. As in the princely courts, the colours would change every year.

Another, more ancient type of identification mark existed in the shape of the crest decorating the helmet, worn of course only in military circles. Warriors wore crests on their helmets in Classical and barbarian times; during the early Middle Ages the crest took the form of tufts of feathers or horns. In the late twelfth century certain seals began to depict flat-based helmets surmounted by heraldic figures in relief. The first example of one of these bore the lion of the Counts of Flanders. The example set by the princes and feudal barons was soon followed: the crest enjoyed rapid and long-lived success, particularly in German-speaking territories, in some areas replacing the shield. It was only ever worn for tournaments, however. Powerful lineages handed down figures borrowed from their coats of arms; sometimes, however, for a festive occasion, individuals would choose a more personal or topical emblem, as would less well-off knights. Humour and imagination were given free reign. Fantastic and exotic creatures from the bestiary were popular, as were themes from romances; some of the emblems used word play, or comic characters or situations. Accounts of jousts held by princes in the fifteenth century describe the participants' helmet crests with as much attention to detail as the illustrations of coats of arms; we learn that they did not consist only of decorations dreamed up by designers – real materials were used as well, fragile constructions made from wood, cardboard and leather, as brightly coloured as were the shields.

EXCLUSION AND DISCRIMINATION

Leprosy, an illness whose ravages inspired extraordinary fear in the Middle Ages, was thought to be contagious. Even though there was a leper king continuing to reign in the East, the unfortunate victims of the disease frequently faced banishment. Lepers were forced to leave their families and employment and to join a group of fellow-sufferers. The organisation of these communities or colonies and their regulations are not known before the thirteenth century, during which their statutes were written down; the isolation of lepers, and the fear among the healthy of contact with sufferers date from much further back. More than their clothing, it is the instrument they carried to signal their presence, a kind of oliphant or horn, that makes them identifiable in early iconography (up to the eleventh century); the wooden rattle made its appearance in the twelfth century.

During the thirteenth century a number of attempts were made to dress lepers in a cape, fastened, or long garments, also fastened. Nevertheless, although an illustration exists of a well-off looking leper wearing shoes, a long gown, a hood covering his shoulders with a wide-brimmed hat on top, there are many more pictures in which the leper, in short clothes like any other man of the people, is identifiable only by his rattle. Some diocese were eager to clothe lepers in a uniform, advocating a garment in off-white wool that strongly resembled a monastic habit. There were no rituals to accompany entry into a leper colony; parts of the funeral service were eventually allowed.

A small group of people in Aquitaine, suffering from symptoms similar to those of leprosy, were rejected by public and authorities alike and had to wear cut-out insignia on their outer garment – sometimes a goose or duck's foot in a contrasting colour. This type of identification mark was not restricted to those suffering from contagious disease or suspected sufferers. Various members of medieval society were subjected to being singled out in this way for religious reasons – non-Christians or semi-repentant heretics – or for moral reasons, like prostitutes. Sometimes a special hat or garment was imposed on 'deviants'.

Well before sumptuary laws were introduced to ensure that a person's position in society was reflected in his dress, the Lateran Council in 1215 ordered bishops to make sure that Jews and Saracens in their provinces wore a distinctive mark on their clothing to differentiate them from Christians. The ostensible reason was the prevention of marriage between Christians and non-Christians on the pretext of ignorance of their different faith. This suggests that in most communities traditional dress had been abandoned and the religious minorities integrated into the Christian environment, until a reaction broke out. The civil authorities had the task of imposing the Churches'

54 *The Alba Bible.* Casa de Alba, Palacio de Liria, Madrid, Vit. I, f.12E, illuminated in Castile *c.*1422–30. A Jew wearing a brightly coloured identifying circle on his right shoulder.

decisions and as a result these took many different forms. The commonest rule was for men to wear a badge cut out of brightly coloured cloth, red most frequently, or yellow or green, or sometimes a combination of red and white, on their outer garment. Such an identification mark was apparently inspired by the one imposed on Christians and Jews in Muslim countries from the seventh century onwards. It was usually in the shape of a circle, sometimes of a specified minimum size, the breadth of a hand. In the Kingdom of Portugal, in the fourteenth century, a half-moon of coloured cloth had to be worn by Muslims and a six-pointed red star by Jews. In England, in 1218, Henry II ordered the wearing of two long bands of white fabric or parchment on the chest, to represent the Tables of the Law. In 1415 a papal bull ruled that Jewish women should wear the identifying circle on their forehead. Generally there had to be two visible bands of blue on the veil worn after marriage. The Jews found these discriminatory marks outrageous and in some instances were able to buy, on an individual basis or for their whole community, exemption from wearing them. The attitude of the authorities was very variable. In a town like Marseilles the rules fell into disuse when the magistrates refused to take any notice of denunciations. Other jurisdictions taxed violations of the law, sometime even confiscating the offending garment.

Certain types of clothing were forbidden to Jews, in particular the great cloak, worn by the aristocracy and members of the clergy. The cost of clothing might be the subject of regulations, as well as the quality of the fabric and even the width of the sleeves or belt. In some places particular dress was imposed on Jews. In Aragon and Castile, the outer garment had to be full-length, elsewhere the hood had to be a special shape. In Rome in the second half of the fourteenth century, Jewish men and women could be identified by their red outer garment. An element of traditional garb (rather than an imposed discrimination), the Jewish hat seems to have been derived from the yellow conical hat worn by non-Muslims in Islamic countries; it was imported to the West by Jews from the East and from Spain. It appeared in France in the eleventh century, in Italy in the twelfth century, and was still worn in its original form in Castile in the middle of the thirteenth century. In Germany and also in England its shape developed to include a brim, large or small, topped by a point which terminated in a bobble. Hebrew manuscripts refrain from illustrating the identification circle, but often represent the hat. German Jews commonly wore it and added it to their coats of arms. It was not until the second half of the thirteenth century that wearing the hat was made obligatory in Austria, Saxony, then Swabia, the Kingdom of Poland and also in Strasbourg. As soon as it had been made obligatory, the hat, hitherto deliberately different from hats worn by Christians, was viewed by Jews in a negative light. The discriminatory nature of the clothing regulations was reinforced by a series of restrictions on Jews which frequently caused their expulsion from a town or kingdom. As time went by the distinctive marks that Jews were forced to wear on their clothing resulted in incidents far removed from the original intention of the legislation; a fifteenth-century legal document states that a Jew can be heavily fined for travelling without wearing the circle and thereby attempting to evade payment of a toll imposed only on Jews.

Christian deviants were also sometimes obliged to wear marks on their clothing that were even more obvious than the Jewish circle. In the early years of the fourteenth century the Inquisition, on sending a Cathar (probably a penitent) home to his village ordered him to wear two yellow felt crosses on all his clothing except his shirt for the

55 Terence: *Comédies*. Musée des Beaux-Arts, Nantes, MS 1665, illuminated in France in the fifteenth century. A prostitute wearing a cloak with elegant scalloped sleeves and a hood with a very long peak.

rest of his life, 'out of hatred of his former ways'. The judgment gives the exact measurement of the crosses in great detail, where they are to be sewn and when they are to be worn. The arms of the cross must measure respectively two palms and two and a half palms in length and two fingers in width; one cross is to be sewn to the back of his robe, 'between the shoulders', the other in front, on the chest. The condemned man was forbidden to appear, inside or outside his house, without the two crosses being visible. Finally, he had a duty to replace them if they became torn or worn out.

A series of legal measures were drawn up in the thirteenth century imposing distinctive clothing on prostitutes, as had been done to Jews. Attempts were made at the time to shut them away in houses or neighbourhoods, but when this was not successful the urban authorities compromised by putting them under the supervision of someone other than the normal town police, and this was sometimes

the town executioner. Although the ostensible intention was to protect the virtue of respectable women, the identifying clothing was
worn by women who could not expect the same protection from
male violence as could normal citizens. To start with, prostitutes were
very visibly marked by special clothing, but this gradually reduced.
The striped cloak worn by prostitutes in Marseilles, the striped hood
worn in England, the white hood of Toulouse, the black and white
pointed hat of Strasbourg were increasingly replaced by bands of fabric stitched to the sleeve or the shoulder, then by tassels worn on the
arm. The prescribed colours were the same as the colours of the
circles worn by Jews: yellow, with its pejorative connotations, the
more ambiguous green, neutral white and even red (in other respects
a well thought of colour); in short, colours that would stand out
against normal clothing. In many towns prostitutes were prohibited
from wearing a headdress or hood, and this set them apart most
strongly: to pull off a woman's headdress amounted to an accusation
of prostitution.

Discriminatory marks were not in use everywhere, however. In
the fifteenth century they appear not to have been imposed in
Florence, Venice or Paris. Clothing regulations for prostitutes were
incorporated into the spirit of the sumptuary laws: costume should be
a reflection of each person's social position and it was not desirable for
prostitutes to look too prosperous. All items of clothing regarded as
luxurious are itemised in the list of forbidden wear: good quality fabrics, fabrics dyed with kermes, fine furs, ornamentation on clothing,
jewellery. In 1360 the very severe provost of Paris forbade prostitutes
to wear embroidery of any kind, pearls, gilt or silver buttons and
squirrel edgings to their clothes. The regulations followed fashions
and the prohibitions increased as fashions developed, making fines
and penalties more severe. The most common penalty was confisca-
tion of the offending garment, but sometimes honour was satisfied if
the garment was altered to comply with the regulations: a cutler
might be called to cut off a pair of squirrel-lined sleeves or shorten a
train. If a silver belt was deemed too extravagant it was simply con-
fiscated.

Outside the courts, police responsible for prostitutes had considerable leeway in exercising their authority. They would sometimes per-
mit women to redeem the obligation of wearing the marks of their
profession, or they might forcibly remove clothing that did not comply; most frequently, however, they were authorised to collect a fine

for each infringement. The position of these women was precarious as a result, because their clothing and jewellery were intended to attract attention and, for them, represented a considerable investment. The value of fabrics and furs, and also of jewellery, allowed them to build up a small amount of capital which arbitrary legislation might deprive them of at any moment. Late thirteenth- and early fourteenth-century regulations stipulated that the sumptuary laws prohibiting decent women from wearing cloth of gold, silk, fine furs and jewellery did not apply to 'venal women'; this may have been designed to protect prostitutes from the risk of losing their finery.

CHAPTER NINE

Beyond Society's Limits

IN WESTERN SOCIETY IN THE MIDDLE AGES, as in all strongly hierarchical societies, elements that threatened its organisation were permitted a voice, but dissent was gradually channelled and modified as
time went by. The evidence for this is scarce, however, and for the
most part late; although the roots of dissent can be discerned in traditional folklore and culture, only vague impressions of its outward
expression, its protagonists and the way it developed during the
medieval period can be gleaned.

CARNIVALS AND POPULAR ENTERTAINMENT

In spite of opposition from the Church, which was ever ready to liken
a masked face to the Devil, disguised the better to tempt mankind, the
tradition of fancy dress persisted. Unfortunately no medieval masks
have survived. Most of the documents describing occasions at which
masks might have been worn were written by scholars, laymen or,
more commonly, clerics who were more interested in castigating
excess than describing its protagonists. The annual celebrations of the
twelve days of Christmas and Carnival were of great importance in
towns in the Middle Ages, giving rise to outbursts of festivity reminiscent of the saturnalia of Classical Rome. The clergy were involved as
well. Choirboys and sacristans, clerics in minor orders such as deacons
and even some fully fledged priests took part in the masquerades which
began in church (even on the altar) before spilling out into the streets.
Games inspired by the theme of 'the world upside down' or 'folly'
were set to traditional dances and music. Power was replaced by anti-
power, under the leadership of a mad king or a mad bishop; all that
was held sacred was then profaned. This was the time for excesses of
food and drink, and obscene and scatalogical pleasantries. Fancy dress
and masks were obligatory, but the authors of contemporary texts did
not waste time describing them.

56   Robert de Borron: *Histoire du Saint Graal et de Merlin.* Bibliothèque Nationale, Paris, Fr. 95, f.261v, illuminated in Picardy *c.*1280. A man disguised as an animal peeps through a hole in the body of his stag costume.

Contemporary iconography is more informative. The margins of vulgate texts, and sometimes more complex illustrations like those accompanying the famous manuscript of the *Roman de Fauvel*, dating from the beginning of the fourteenth century, depict small masked figures, dressed up for a charivari and drawn from life. There are two main themes. The 'upside down' theme is sometimes expressed as cross-dressing, men dressed as women, or, more crudely, as clothes worn back to front, often indecently revealing parts of the body. Dressing as animals was a favourite pastime. The preachers of the early Middle Ages were correct in saying that such traditions went back to pagan times. The wild animals preferred included the bear, the wild boar, the monkey, the deer, the eagle, the hare; domestic animals were not despised – bull, goat, calf, ram, lamb and donkey accompany their wild brethren. The disguise sometimes consisted only of a mask covering the face, or a whole head, with ears and, at a later date, characteristic horns; it could be worn balanced on the shoulders or attached to a full-length *housse*.

Charivaris were popular entertainments put on by well-organised groups of male actors generally to celebrate the remarriage of a widow or widower. As if the opposite of an aubade, they evoked the world of the dead with a cacophany of sound – kitchen equipment such as saucepan lids, pans, kettles and bells of all sizes; the people involved sometimes caused annoyance and violence might break out. As in the festivals of fools, in charivaris verbal battles would be unleashed and obscene gestures abounded. Women might be the victims but did not take part. If the drawings in the margins of a copy of a *Roman d'Alexandre* are to be believed, women danced in a more sedate fashion, without fancy dress, next to the masked men. One of these pictures possibly depicts a *carole* being danced; the men are masked and dressed in shapeless clothes, the women in simple gowns, with veils. In another picture, two *farandoles* are danced simultaneously, men on one side, women on the other.

FANCY DRESS AND COURTLY GAMES

The details of the last-mentioned miniature painting suggest that the men with their features concealed by animal heads belong to the ruling class. They are dressed in short gowns and each has a dagger attached to a broad belt; coats of arms can be spotted on one or two of the little capes covering their shoulders – probably capes attached to the hoods worn under the masks. The low-necked, fitted gowns of the young women dancing opposite them, bare headed, would also appear to belong to the fashions reserved for the upper classes. By the end of the Middle Ages, the taste for masked, fancy dress entertainments had spread to the royal courts. One of the most favoured subjects was the 'wild man', characterised by his nakedness and his abundant hairiness. To portray this creature the actors at first slipped on an animal skin, but later tight clothing with hanks of tow or dried moss stitched all over it created a more sophisticated impression. These outfits were highly inflammable and cost the lives of several courtiers who, in 1393, were dressed up for a charivari, later remembered as the Burning Ball (Bal des Ardents) during which Charles VI of France narrowly escaped being burnt to death. Wild men, women and children continued to crop up in the fifteenth century, in decoration and in clothing where they can be found amidst the devices and crests. Fashionable youth used the theme of the wild man for their festivities. One of the fine tapestries in Saumur recalls such masquerades: young women dressed as 'wild' women mingle with the other young people. They are still wearing their usual finery and floating veils and their fancy dress is partly hidden by their huge gathered cloaks.

At the festivals held at court to celebrate the first of May the dressing up was much more discreet; these rituals were observed by almost the entire population and clearly belonged to a tradition far back in folk history. The courtiers (and probably the peasants as well) would go out and gather greenery from which they would weave crowns and belts, before returning to the castle to carry on with festivities there. Even rulers who had achieved a certain age would have green clothing tailored for the occasion – the only time when they would wear this colour, which symbolised youth and the uncertainties of love.

Royal account books contain evidence of purchases for fancy dress entertainments of a much more elaborate nature, though it is not always possible to connect these with a particular festival. In 1332 masks or 'false faces', with dishevelled hair made of silk, were supplied to the lords and ladies of the court of Artois, with long gowns suited to either sex. The rulers did not take part personally in these festivities but enjoyed providing the opportunity for dancing the *moresca* as often as possible in the fifteenth century. The name of these dances, derived from the name given to converted Moors in Spain, suggests an oriental origin. The clothing worn, and the activities engaged in, differed enormously. At the court of René d'Anjou, in Provence, the young princesses and the queen's handmaidens received simple 'surplices', long tunics of fine linen, to dance a *moresca* before the king. At the court of France, the five 'gentlemen and officers' assigned to the amusement of Charles VII on the evening of Shrove Tuesday in 1459 were encased in floor-length garments, half white and half green; the large quantity of silk muslin ordered for the headdresses leaves little doubt that they must have been wearing turbans.

The opulence and exotic colour of the Islamic world were highly valued in Western court circles and exercised a fascination that may have owed something to the spirit of the crusades. Besides fancy dress, actors were recruited; 'black Moors' and 'white Moors', in the terminology of the day, were the African slaves frequently to be found in countries bordering the Mediterranean, but also present in more northerly countries. René d'Anjou liked clothing his Moors in colours that stood out against the colours worn by his other servants. He designed brightly coloured but simple clothing for them in woollen cloth of mediocre quality. Red and 'turkey blue' for the older ones, 'gay green' and blue for the younger ones, to be worn alternately with less vivid outfits. Sometimes a particular style stands out, for example jackets with dagged points or the 'Saracen robes' bought specially for them. For special parades they would occasionally be dressed in silk. During the jousts that went by the name of the Ascendancy of the Joyful Guard (Emprises de la Joyeuse Garde), where they led the parade of combatants, they were dressed in the Turkish style – long caftans with red and white damask turbans, and each with a lion on a lead. A 'fool', also dressed as a Turk, is seen sitting cross-legged beside them when they stood still to form a tableau.

From the Juggler to the King's Fool

Whether they were mimes, musicians, acrobats, animal trainers, real jugglers or minstrels, performers were always called *jongleurs* or 'actors' by the town clerks. In the twelfth and thirteenth centuries the latter justified their rejection of suspicious or marginal characters on religious grounds; groups of vagrants or itinerants worried them. The terms of their reproach were the same as their reproaches to participants in the annual Carnival: masks and fancy dress were deprecated, as were physical deformities (if they were exploited), gesticulation (immobility was considered a sign of control of the passions) and, finally, disorderly language. As far as clothing went, on the other hand, the censors seem to have reserved their criticism solely for fancy dress. Was the role of witness assigned to the miniature painters? Some of the wandering actors are indeed portrayed wearing extraordinary clothing, from their shoes to their headdress by way of the stripes on their costume. These early representations probably express society's negative view of the wearers of the clothing rather than any accurate picture of the costume itself. The broad stripes, in particular, were as pejorative as the broad stripes in heraldry, particularly if the colour yellow was predominant.

As time passed the group of performers began to diversify, some members specialising and gaining a stable position in society. Musicians in particular banded together in towns and the local prince would try to attract the best of them to his court. The costumes worn by some of the instrumental groups (often including women) portrayed in the fourteenth century show great imagination: they were frequently quartered and cut from striped fabrics, with narrow or

57   *Scene at a Tournament* (detail). Musée des Beaux-Arts, Tours, painted in
Florence in the mid-fifteenth century. The musicians accompanying the jousting are wearing extravagant costumes in bright contrasting colours.

broad stripes, in light, bright colours. To perform, they borrowed the
finery worn by the nobility. Like princes, municipal authorities used
sometimes to hire the services of musicians. For traditional festivals
they would have clothes made for them in the same colours that they
had chosen that year for the rest of their retinue. In Dijon, in the early
years of the fifteenth century, the town hall distributed quartered
clothing to the minstrels who played in the streets in the evenings
during Advent; one year the outfits were quartered in green and
stripes, the next year in red and black. Later, in the mid-fifteenth
century, the posthumous inventory of a very modest town musician
reveals that he possessed only multi-coloured clothing. These costumes were not worn simply for playing; they represent a manner of
dressing that was like a trade mark. This particular musician had two
outfits, one in blue and green wool, the other in blue and red; he
might have received them as part of a distribution or possibly he
bought them cheaply, second hand, from someone's livery. His two
black *chaperons* bore little coloured horns, unlike anything worn by
the rest of the citizenry, one of them red and black, the other green.
Fifteenth-century painting contains many allusions to groups of
military musicians: these consisted mainly of trumpeters wearing

58 *Bromholm   Psalter*. Bodleian   Library,
Oxford, Ashmole 1523, f.66, illuminated in the
east of England *c*.1300. The fool wears a blue
tunic over bare legs, and a pink hood with three
points, each with a small bell on top. The
emblem of his profession is a bladder.

gowns decorated with the device of the prince they served when they
played at tournaments, official entries and at banquets.

Fools followed more closely in the footsteps of *jongleurs* than did
musicians. A fool was a professional entertainer who drew on the
tradition of mime as well as the 'sot' or idiot; he was an ambiguous
character whose remarks often meant the reverse of what they
appeared to mean, entertaining and admonishing at the same time.
The fool's clothing, with its special accessories, evolved very slowly
as money and the spirit of imitation permitted. Illustrations of the
thirteenth to fifteenth centuries allow us to chart its course and show
how dwarfs and the deformed gradually adopted the role of the fool,
quite late and particularly in court circles. The specific costume
feature of the fool was his hood, sometimes worn on its own. At first
this was simply a long pointed hat with a bell on the end; donkeys'
ears were added later, plus a large number of little bells. The short,
loose tunic of the early fourteenth century became a tight-fitting
jacket with dagged hem. Green and yellow were not the only colours
worn; innumerable illustrations show red, blue and even grey in
combination with yellow, green or indeed each other. The disorderly
impression was accentuated by hose of different colours, and a motley
hood – with diamonds or a chequerboard of squares – similar to the
familiar heraldic designs. The primitive emblem of the fool was a
club, bladder or a whip, but this gradually developed into an effigy of
the fool at the end of a stick, the fool's bauble. Female fools cropped

up occasionally in the courts of the late Middle Ages, and there were child fools as well. It is not known if they also wore asses' ears on their heads, but the clothing bought for them was brightly coloured and probably variegated as well if the name 'Many-coloured Madam' given to one of the female fools of the day is a reliable guide.

PROCESSIONS AND PARADES

Processions and parades ought, by right, to have been a faithful reflection of the proprieties and hierarchies as conceived by clerics and princes. Unfortunately the importance attached to the visual aspects of religion, and of the relationship between urban and princely authorities, was so great that it led to additions to the ceremonial – exaggerated fancy dress and highly theatrical elements.

Religious processions, already containing choir boys, clerics, priests and later ecclesiastical dignitaries of the most elevated rank, also sometimes included children disguised as angels. A simple pair of wings could be worn on top of a white tunic; the 'angel's costume' mentioned in some inventories of the possessions of townsfolk is unfortunately never described more fully. During the Middle Ages the custom also arose of introducing edifying scenes from the lives of the saints into church processions. Even if the person lucky enough to represent the saint was dressed in normal clothing, proceedings could be enlivened by the introduction of mythical monsters, embodiments of evil, conquered or tamed by the saint in question. 'Processional dragons', animated by several people, belonged to the category of fancy dress. They were far less localised than the Provençal version, the tarasque, which can still be seen in certain towns in Provence. Town councils financed the making of these beasts very generously and sometimes procured fine silk to cover them.

As the Middle Ages drew to a close a darker side of religious fervour appeared in processions in the form of 'penitents' or 'flagellants'. These men belonged to religious associations or brotherhoods and wore clothes similar to monastic habits but hid their faces under conical cowls. Some of them whipped themselves as they processed, or displayed the wounds they had inflicted upon themselves through openings in the backs of their tunics. The charitable brotherhoods were less extreme in their public displays of fervour; they also

59   *Missel-Heures franciscain.* Bibliothèque Nationale, Paris, Lat. 757, f.155, illuminated in Lombardy in 1385. Religious procession: behind the cowled flagellants, whose robes leave their backs bare, clergy in surplices precede the cardinals, with the Pope bringing up the rear.

processed, however, each group behind the banner of their association. In honour of their patron saint, members would wear their best clothes (not uniform), sometimes with insignia to demonstrate their allegiance.

The same people would appear, albeit less frequently, when sovereigns made solemn entries into a town. These parades were definitely secular. The religious authorities would wait in the church for the king to come and make his devotions. This was when ordinary citizens had a chance to appear in a parade, as members of trade guilds or office holders in the local administration. The meeting with the visiting sovereign would take place outside the city, often a long way out. In troubled times an armed division of crossbowmen would lead the parade. In some towns a group of children carrying small banners or branches headed the march, in front of the town magistrates. After them came the guilds behind their standards, lined up in strict order with the noblest trades at the front: money changers, drapers, grocers etc. At the back of the procession came the inn-keepers. In the second half of the fourteenth century the tradition arose of uniform clothing, each paying for his own. Although the documents never make it absolutely clear, it seems probable that only better-off citizens were involved, those belonging to the élite of their profession; the purchase of coloured fabrics for such occasions was beyond the reach of the main bulk of the population. The chief aim was to flatter the visiting sovereign. The colours worn were usually the brightest: red, blue, green. Vivid contrasts were sought in the colours of the quarters, or between the gowns and the hoods. When white was chosen, very exceptionally, as it was for the entry of Charles VII into Tournai in 1464, the chronicler makes it plain that it was to demonstrate the humility of the city towards its ruler. To express their attachment to the king even more unmistakably the 'three hundred notables' added two large fleurs-de-lis embroidered in silk to their costumes, one on the chest and one on the back. The welcome parade was composed exclusively of men; the women were stationed in the square outside the main church, while the clergy waited inside. The sovereign's retinue, consisting of his relations and highest dignitaries, plus their squires, also consisted entirely of men, unless there should be a newly wed or newly crowned queen to greet. In the twelfth and thirteenth centuries royal entries in England and the Holy Roman Empire were recorded by chroniclers; the ritual betrays its two sources, on one hand the official welcome or triumph extended to rulers in Classical times, on the other the memory of Jesus Christ's triumphal entry into Jerusalem. Detailed descriptions of the ceremonial from the end of the fourteenth and the early fifteenth centuries make it clear that kings would wear their royal robes for such an occasion. In all surviving records of royal entries, the King of France is attired in blue silk vestments embroidered in gold thread with fleurs-de-lis; the lily motif is repeated on the canopy commissioned by the city authorities to cover the monarch's head.

All the descriptions confirm that musicians were present to provide a musical accompaniment to proceedings, sometimes being clothed for the occasion at the city's expense. After the early decades of the fourteenth century, choreographic entertainments were also offered to important guests at the gates of a number of towns in Provence. A meal would always be offered after the ceremonial, followed by dancing. The *tableaux vivants* that punctuated the sovereign's route into town were intended to welcome him with messages of allegiance. When Charles VII visited Rouen after its recapture in 1449 he met a 'woman symbolising the town, on her knees with her hands joined'; she was surrounded by representatives of the Church, the nobility and the bourgeoisie; farther on two young women were holding a large white deer, the king's emblem. At the gate through which the same king entered the town of Tournai there was a young woman seated in a 'castle' (symbolising the town) holding in her hands a golden heart, which she opened just as the sovereign passed, revealing the fleur-de-lis inside, the symbol of the town's loyalty to their ruler.

TOWARDS THEATRICAL COSTUME

Tableaux vivants and 'mysteries' had been popular in towns for centuries; the organisers of royal visits included them in their programmes. The relatively large sums of money available on these occasions permitted them to commission elaborate equipment for special effects and have proper theatrical costumes made. Unfortunately the chroniclers of Charles VII's visit to Tournai

60   Terence: *Comédies*. Bibliothèque Nationale, Paris, Lat. 7907 A, f.2v, illuminated in Paris *c*.1407–12. Except for their masks, the actors are dressed exactly like the audience.

considered the eighteen scenes enacted on platforms, at street corners and in squares too lengthy to describe in detail; the subjects of the drama were Charlemagne, Clovis and Saint Louis, and 'other mysteries that have taken place since the time of the first man, Adam'.

A few descriptions survive of the fine fabrics in all the colours of the rainbow, decorated with beaten gold, used to clothe the women personifying the cardinal virtues or, for another royal visit, the men and women representing the Nine Valiant Men and the Nine Valiant Women. Sometimes the list of expenses incurred in preparation for a royal entry provides more detailed information on the materials used to make the costumes. The composition of two costumes for wild men made in Lyons in 1389 before Charles vi's first visit there are a case in point: gowns, hoods and hose were made up from strong linen by a tailor, then sent on to a woman who stitched moss and irises all over them. More elaborate costumes are also documented, for example those for mermaids gambolling in fountains. The surviving information, scanty though it is, suggests that the fabrics used for these one-off performances were not very costly, but that the trimmings of beaten gold or silver leaf, in imitation of cloth of gold or silver, aimed at maximum effect. All then was illusion, a glimpse into a fantasy world that, while the festivities went on, fed the public imagination with its beauty and colour.

Conclusion

THE EVER INCREASING IMPORTANCE given to primary source material has played a crucial role in recent developments in research into medieval costume. Greatly improved study of iconography and the analysis of economic and technical documents as well as archaeological finds have enormously extended our understanding of what raw materials were available during the period and of how they were used. As a result of the development of cloth manufacture, with concomitant technical improvements throughout that process – hence also the development of silk production in the south and the expansion of the fur trade – purchasers were offered an increasingly great choice in the matter of materials, as well as a stream of new products. The methods whereby clothing was procured also witnessed great change. As urban workshops sprang up, estate and domestic production gradually decreased as specialists took over. The system of gifts and distributions, embedded in Christian ideology as well as in the social structure of feudal society, did not, however, disappear at this juncture.

As far as clothing was concerned, the speed and nature of change was based on wealth and social position and therefore varied widely. The vast majority of the populace, in the region of ninety per cent, belonged to the peasant class; peasants and the urban poor constituted a working class whose clothing was essentially utilitarian and changed only very slowly. Even when adaptations were made to accommodate climatic conditions or the requirements of different types of labour, these were made with limited resources and solutions that were generally of the simplest; a few items of genuine working clothing began to make their appearance. The driving force behind change was to be found at the other end of the social scale among monarchs and warriors, who held political power and disposed of very considerable wealth. The moral code of the chivalrous class considered largesse a cardinal virtue and encouraged its members to set themselves apart from the rest of the populace by the brilliance of their

appearance. The increasing popularity of the short, fairly fitted clothing worn by those who rode horses was, for a while, eclipsed by the
long billowing tunics favoured by southern Europeans. Finally, however, the short costume in two pieces won the day for the laity,
though it would sometimes be amplified by a long gown or a mantle
to give dignity. The social significance of clothing, undocumented in
the early Middle Ages, was made crystal clear by the sumptuary laws
towards the end of the period. Economic motives were of less importance to the authors of the law than the concern to accord each individual a rightful place in society. Even a royal princess might be liable
to some restrictions on the extravagance of her dress; women never
shared their husband's rank, whatever social class thay belonged to,
and at least in aristocratic society, this subordination had an influence
on the way they dressed. At other social levels women appear sometimes to have dressed more elegantly: working-class women wore
coloured fabrics with greater frequency, perhaps on account of the
types of activity in which they were engaged. Increase in travel and
family visits between royal and princely courts (wars and dynastic
quarrels permitting) help to explain the gradual spread of most male
fashions all over the Western world. Regional differences, more
obvious in female than male fashion, can be explained by lesser par-
ticipation in travel and fewer international contacts.

The full significance of clothing went further than the mere defi-
nition of social class, gender or regional difference. While attitudes to
nakedness and states of undress revealed a high degree of consensus,
as did variations in clothing according to age, there were deep divisions in attitudes to personal status, whether inherited, acquired or
chosen. Distinctive features of a more and more elaborate kind multiplied on clothing and accessories, proving the medieval sensitivity to
visual signs and also the medieval taste for encoding people and situations. On the other hand working-class clothing bore few distinctive
signs. The extravagance of the clothing worn by religious functionar-
ies, little changed since the sixth century, had a strong influence on
what was worn by kings and emperors at their coronations, all
intended to exalt and enhance the dignity of the rulers. Conversely
monks and friars, who had renounced the world, expressed their
renunciation in simple clothing or sometimes, in some of the orders,
in clothing pushed to exaggerated extremes of poverty. Similarly the
insignia procuring positive recognition for knights, crusaders, pilgrims and (later) the orders of chivalry contrasted with the negative

marks imposed on 'deviants' from the prevalent religious and moral codes. From the thirteenth century Jews, Muslims and heretics were made to wear distinguishing markers on their clothing. The fate of the prostitute, left to the discretion of local urban authorities, was more variable. Sufferers from the only illness recognised as contagious, leprosy, were restricted to a few areas and, very late in the day, forced into distinctive garments; more usually it was an accessory, noisy and very visible, that heralded their arrival and frightened others away. There were times and places however when Western society in the Middle Ages escaped from societal constraints and conventions. Carnivals and charivaris had a certain anarchic quality, sometimes expressed quite violently and in extraordinary garb. In courtly surroundings, however, although still inspired by the idea of the world upside down, and redolent with animal disguises which had emerged from the remains of paganism, fancy dress was enjoyed at a more refined level even though the theme of the wild man continued to be particularly popular. On a daily basis, the brilliantly coloured, exotic clothing of Moorish slaves, of fools (both men and women) and minstrels created a milieu for the courts in which imagination and fantasy had free rein. On a similar note, behind the expressions of loyalty and allegiance, parades and processions staged by towns in honour of a royal visit embodied the rising power of the urban aristocracy.

BIBLIOGRAPHY

Actes du premier congrès international d'histoire du costume (Venice, 1952), Milan, Centro internazionale delle arti e del costume, 1955.

Aubailly, Jean-Claude, *Le Théâtre médiéval profane et comique, la naissance d'un art*, Paris, Larousse, 1975.

Barthes, Roland, *Système de la mode*, Paris, Le Seuil, 1969 (new edn, Paris, Le Seuil, 1983).

Beaulieu, Michèle, 'Le Costume de deuil en Bourgogne au xve siècle', in *Actes du xviie congrès international de l'art* (Amsterdam, 1952), The Hague, 1955.

Beaulieu, Michèle et Baylé, Jeanne, *Le Costume de Bourgogne de Philipe Le Hardi à la mort de Charles Le Téméraire (1364–1477)*, Paris, P.U.F., 1956.

Beaune, Colette, 'Costume et pouvoir en France à la fin du Moyen Âge: les devises royales vers 1400', *Revue des Sciences Humaines*, 55 (no. 183), 1981, pp. 125–46.

Bériac, Françoise, *Histoire des lépreux au Moyen Âge*, Paris, Imago, 1988.

Bernis Madrazo, Carmen, *Indumentaria medieval española*, Madrid, Istituto Diego Velasquez, 1956.

Bernis, Carmen, *Trajes y modas en la España de los Reyes Católicos*, Madrid, Istituto Diego Velasquez, 2 vols, 1970.

Blair, Claude, *European Armour circa 1066 to circa 1700*, London, Batsford, 1958.

Blanc, Odile, 'Les Stratégies de la parure dans le divertissement chevaleresque (xve siècle)', *Communications*, 46, 1987, pp. 49–65.

Borlandi, Franco, 'Futainiers et futaines en Italic au Moyen Âge', in *Éventail de l'histoire vivante, hommage à Lucien Febvre*, Paris, A. Colin, vol. 2, 1953, pp. 133–40.

Boucher, François *Histoire du costume en Occident de l'Antiquité à nos jours*, Paris, Flammarion, 1965 (new edn, Paris, Flammarion, 1983).

Bourilly, Joseph, *Le Costume en Provence au Moyen Âge*, Marseilles, Institut historique de Provence, 1929.

Braudel, Fernand, *Civilisation matérielle, économie et capitalisme*, Paris, A. Colin, 1967 (new edn, Paris, A. Colin, 1988).

Bridbury, A. R., *Medieval English Clothmaking. An Economic Survey*, London, Heinemann Educational, 1982.

Bulst, Neithard, 'Zum Problem Städtischer und Territorialer Kleider, Aufwands und Luxusgesetzgebung in Deutschland (13.–Mitte 16. Jahrhundert)' in *Renaissance du pouvoir législatif et genèse de l'état*, Montpellier, Publication de la Société d'Histoire du Droit, 1988, pp. 29–57.

Bulst, Neithard, 'La Législation somptuaire d'Amédée viii', *Amédée viii–Félix v, Premier duc de Savoie et pape, 1383–1451* (Colloque Ripaille-Lausanne), Lausanne, ed. B. Andenmatten and A. Paravicini Bagliani, 1992, pp. 191–200.

Buttin, François, *Du costume militaire au Moyen Âge et pendant la Renaissance*, Barcelona, Real Academia de Buenas Letras, 1971.

Cahiers Ciba (Les), Basle, 1946–70.

Cappi Bentivegna, Ferrucia, *Abbigliamento e costume nella pittura italiana*, Rome, F. Cappi Bentivegna, vol. 1, 1962.

Cardon, Dominique, 'Echantillons de draps de laine des archives Datini (fin XIVe début XVe siècle). Analyses techniques, importance historique', in *Mélanges de l'École Française de Rome (MEFREM)*, 103 (1), 1991, pp. 359–72.

Cardon, Dominique and Du Châtenet, Gaëtan, *Guide des teintures naturelles*, Neufchâtel-Paris, Delachaux and Nestlié, 1990.

Casagrande, Carla and Vecchio, Silvana, 'Clercs et jongleurs dans la société médiévale (XIIe–XIIIe siècles)', *Annales ESC*, 34e année (no. 5), 1979, pp. 913–28.

Le Charivari, (ed. Jacques Le Goff and Jean-Claude Schmitt), Paris-The Hague-New York, Mouton, 1981.

Ciba Review, Basle, 1937–.

Closson, Monique, Mane, Perrine and Piponnier, Françoise, 'Le Costume paysan au Moyen Âge: sources et méthodes', *Vêtements et sociétés* (Actes des journées de rencontre des 2 et 3 mars 1979), Paris, 1981, pp. 161–70.

Cloth and Clothing in Medieval Europe: Essays in Memory of E. M. Carus-Wilson, ed. N. B. Harte and K. G. Ponting, London, Heinemann and Pasold Research Fund, 1982.

Colas, René, *Bibliographie générale du costume et de la mode*, Paris, René Colas, 2 vols, 1933.

Contamine, Philippe, 'L'Ordre de Saint Michel au temps de Louis XI et de Charles VIII', *Bulletin de la Société Nationale des Antiquaires de France*, 1976, pp. 212–38.

Contamine, Philippe, *La Vie quotidienne pendant la guerre de Cent Ans: France et Angleterre, XIVe siècle*, Paris, Hachette, 1976.

Le Corps masqué, Razo, 6, Nice, University of Nice, 1986.

Le Corps paré: ornements et atours, Razo, 7, Nice, University of Nice, 1987.

Costume, London, 1967–.

Coulet, Noël, 'Les Entrées solennelles en Provence au XIVe siècle', *Ethnologie française*, 7 (new ser.), 1977, pp. 63–82.

Crowfoot, Elizabeth, Pritchard, Frances and Staniland, Kay, *Textiles and Clothing*, London, HMSO (Medieval finds from excavations in London, no. 4), 1992.

Cunnington, Cecil Willett and Phyllis, *The History of Underclothes*, London, Michael Joseph, 1951.

Delort, Robert, *Le Commerce des fourrures en Occident à la fin du Moyen Âge: vers 1300–vers 1450*, Rome, École Française de Rome (Bibliothèque des Écoles Françaises d'Athènes et de Rome, 236), 2 vols, 1978.

Delort, Robert, 'Les Animaux et l'habillement', in *L'uomo di fronte al mondo animale nell'alto Medioevo, XXXI settimane di studio sull'alto Medioevo di Spoleto*, Spoleto, 1983, pp. 673–700.

Delort, Robert, 'Fibres textiles et plantes tinctoriales', in *L'ambiente vegetale nell'alto Medioevo, XXXVII settimane di studio sull'alto Medioevo di Spoleto*, Spoleto, 1990, pp. 821–61.

Demay, Germain, *Le Costume au Moyen Âge d'après les sceaux*, Paris, Dumoulin, 1880 (new edn, Paris, Berger-Levrault, 1978).

De Poerck, Guy, *La Draperie médiévale en Flandres et en Artois. Technique et terminologie*, Bruges, De Tempel, 3 vols, 1951.

Deslandres, Yvonne, *Le Costume, image de l'homme*, Paris, Albin Michel, 1976.

Douët d'Arcq, Louis-Claude, *Comptes de l'argenterie des rois de France au XIVe siècle*, Paris,

Renouard, 1851.

Douët d'Arcq, Louis-Claude, *Nouveau Recueil des comptes de l'argenterie des rois de France*, Paris, Renouard, 1884.

Douët d'Arcq, Louis-Claude, *Choix de pièces inédites relatives au règne de Charles VI*, Paris, Société de l'Histoire de France, 2 vols, 1863–4.

Drobnà, Zoroslova, Durbik, Jan and Wagner, Eduard, *Tracht Wehr und Waffen des späten Mittelalters (1350–1450)*, Prague, Artia, 1957.

Egan, Geof and Pritchard, Frances, *Dress Accessories (c. 1150–c. 1450)*, London, HMSO (Medieval finds from excavations in London, no. 3), 1991.

Eisenbart, L. C., *Kleiderordnungen der deutschen Städte zwischen 1350 und 1700. Ein Beitrag zur Kulturgeschichte des deutschen Bürgertums*, Göttingen, 1962.

Enlart, Camille, *Manuel d'archéologie française depuis les temps mérovingiens jusqu'à la Renaissance*, vol. 3: *Le Costume*, Paris, A. Picard, 1916.

Evans, Joan, *Dress in Mediaeval France*, Oxford, Clarendon Press, 1952.

Fillitz, R., *Trésor sacré et profane*, Vienna, Kunsthistorisches Museum, 1963.

Fingerlin, Ilse, *Gürtel des hohen und späten Mittelalters*, Munich-Berlin, Deutscher Kunstverlag, 1971.

Fournier, Jacques, *Le Registre d'Inquisition de Jacques Fournier, Évêque de Pamiers (1318–1325)*, (trans. Jean Duvernoy), Paris-The Hague-New York, Mouton, 3 vols, 1978.

Gay, Victor and Stein, Henri, *Glossaire archéologique du Moyen Âge et de la Renaissance*, Paris, Librairie de la société bibliographique, 2 vols, 1887–1929.

Geremek, Bronislaw, *Les Marginaux parisiens aux xive et xve siècles*, Paris, Flammarion, 1976 (new edn, Paris, Flammarion, 1990).

Gerschel, Lucien, 'Couleur et teinture chez divers peuples indo-européens', *Annales ESC*, 21e année (no. 3), 1966, pp. 608–31.

Goffman, Erving, *La Mise en scène de la vie quotidienne. La présentation de soi*, Paris, Minuit, 1973.

Grew, Francis and De Neergaard, Margarethe, *Shoes and Patters*, London, HMSO (Medieval finds from excavations in London, no. 2), 1988.

Groenman-van Waateringe, W., 'Society Rests on Leather', *Rotterdam Papers*, 2, 1975, pp. 23–34.

Guenée, Bernard and Lehoux, Françoise, *Les Entrées royales françaises de 1328 à 1515*, Paris, CNRS, 1968.

Hargreaves-Mawdsley, W. N., *A History of Academical Dress in Europe until the End of the Eighteenth Century*, Oxford, 1963.

Harmand, Adrien, *Jeanne d'Arc, ses costumes, son armure. Essai de reconstitution*, Paris, Ernest Leroux, 1929.

Heers, Jacques, *Fêtes, jeux et joutes dans les sociétés d'Occident à la fin du Moyen Âge*, Paris, J. Vrin, 1971.

Heers, Jaques, 'La Mode et le marché des draps de laine: Gênes et la Montagne à la fin du Moyen Âge', *Annales ESC*, 26e année (no. 5), 1971, p. 1093–117.

Heers, Jaques, *Fêtes des fous et carnavals*, Paris, Fayard, 1993.

Herrero Carretero, Concha, *Museo de tela medievales. Monasterio de Santa Maria la Real de Huelgas Burgos*, Madrid, Editorial Patrimonio Nacional, 1988.

Hiler, Hilaire and Meyer, Bibliography of Costume. *A Dictionary Catalog of about Eight Thousand Books and Periodicals*, New York, Adah V. Morris, 1965.

Kühnel, Harry et al., *Alltag im Spätmittelalter*, Graz-Vienna-Cologne, Kaleidoscop., 1986.

Kühnel, Harry et al., *Bildwörterbuch der Kleidung und Rüstung*, Stuttgart, Alfred Kröner, 1992.

Kybalová, Ludmila, Herbenová, Olga and Lamarová, Milen, *Encyclopédie illustrée du costume et de la mode*, Paris, Gründ, 1970 (new edn, Paris, Gründ, 1980).

Laporte, Jean-Pierre, *Le Trésor des saints de Chelles*, Chelles, Société archéologique et historique de Chelles, 1988.

La Roncière, Charles de, 'La Vie privée des notables toscans au seuil de la Renaissance', in *Histoire de la vie privée*, ed. P. Ariès and G. Duby, Paris, Le Seuil, vol. 1, 1985, pp. 163–309.

Le Goff, Jacques, 'Aspects religieux et sacrés de la monarchie française du xe au xiiie siècle', in *La Royauté sacrée dans le monde chrétien*, Paris, E.H.E.S.S., 1992, p.19–28.

Lever, Maurice, *Le Sceptre et la marotte: histoire des fous de Cour*, Paris, Fayard, 1983.

Levi-Pisetzky, Rosita, *Storia del costume in Italia*, Milan, Istituto Editoriale Italiano, vols 2–3, 1964.

Levis May, Florence, *Silk Textiles of Spain (Eighth–Fifteenth Century)*, New York, Hispanic Society of America, 1957.

Lombard, Maurice, *Études d'économie médiévale. Les textiles dans le monde musulman du viie au xiie siècle*, Paris-The Hague-New York, Mouton, 1978.

Lunquist, Eva Rodhe, *La Mode et son vocabulaire. Quelques termes de la mode féminine au Moyen Âge, suivis dans leur évolution sémantique*, Göteborg, Wettergren och Kerber, 1950.

Madou, Mireille, *Le Costume civil*, Turnhout, Brepols (Typologie des sources du Moyen Âge occidental, no. 47), 1986.

Mane, Perrine, *Calendriers et techniques agricoles (France-Italie, xiie–xiiie siècles)*, Paris, Le Sycomore, 1981.

Mathew, Gervas, *The Court of Richard ii*, London, John Murray, 1968.

Mayo, J., *A History of Ecclesiastical Dress*, London, Batsford, 1984.

Mazouer, Charles, 'Théâtre et carnaval en France jusqu'à la fin du xvie siècle', *Revue de la société d'histoire du théâtre*, 35, 1983, pp. 147–61.

Mazzi, Maria Serena and Raveggi, Sergio, *Gli uomini e le cose nelle campagne fiorentine del Quattrocento*, Florence, Leo S. Olschki, 1983.

Metzger, Thérèse and Mendel, *La Vie juive au Moyen Âge*, Fribourg, Office du Livre et Paris, Vilo, 1982.

Mille ans de costume français (950–1950), Longwy, G. Klopp, 1991.

Montalto, Lina, *La corte di Alfonso i di Aragona*, Naples, R. Ricciardi, 1922.

Newton, Stella Mary, *Renaissance Theater Costume and the Sense of the Historic Past*, London, Rapp and Whiting, 1975.

Newton, Stella Mary, *Fashion in the Age of the Black Prince. A Study of the Years 1340–1365*, Woodbridge, 1980.

Nordlund, Paul, *Dragt udgivet*, Stockholm, A. Bonniers, 1941.

Oakes, Alma and Hill, Margot Hamilton, *Rural Costume. Its Origin and Development in Western Europe and the British Isles*, London, Batsford, 1970.

Opera textilia variorum temporum to Honour Agnes Geijer on her Ninetieth Birthday (2 Oct. 1988), eds I. Estham and N. Niockert, Stockholm, Statens Historiska Museum, 1988.

Ott, André G., *Études sur les couleurs en vieux français*, Paris, E. Bouillon, 1899.

Page, Agnès, *Vêtir le Prince. Tissus et couleurs à la cour de Savoie (1427–1447)*, Lausanne, Section d'Histoire (Cahiers Lausannois d'histoire médiévale, 8), 1993.

Parisse, Michel, *Les Nonnes au Moyen Âge*, Paris, C. Bonneton, 1983.

Pastoureau, Michel, *Traité d'héraldique*, Paris, Picard, 1979 (new edn, Paris, Picard, 1993).

Pastoureau, Michel, *Figures et couleurs. Étude sur la symbolique et la sensibilité médiévales*, Paris, Le Léopard d'Or, 1986.

Pastoureau, Michel, *Couleurs, images, symboles. Études d'histoire et d'anthropologie*, Paris, Le Léopard d'Or, 1989.

Pastoureau, Michel, 'Ceci est mon sang. Le christianisme médiéval et la couleur rouge', in *Le Pressoir mystique*, Paris, Du Cerf, 1990, pp. 43–56.

Pastoureau, Michel, *L'Étoffe du diable: une histoire des rayures et des tissus rayés*, Paris, Le Seuil, 1991.

Petraschek-Heim, Ingeborg, *Die Sprache der Kleidung, Wesen und Wandel von Tracht, Mode, Kostüm und Uniform*, Vienna, 1966.

Piponnier, Françoise, *Costume et vie sociale. La cour d'Anjou, XIVe–XVe, siècle*, Paris-The Hague-Mouton, 1970.

Piponnier, Françoise, 'Le Costume nobiliaire en France au bas Moyen Âge', in *Adelige Sachkultur des Spätmittelalters*, Vienna, Österreichischen Akademie der Wissenschaften, 1982, pp. 343–63.

Piponnier, Françoise, 'Linge de maison et linge de corps au Moyen Âge d'après les inventaires bourguignons', *Ethnologie française*, 3, 1986, pp. 239–48.

Piponnier, Françoise, 'Matières premières du costume et groupes sociaux. Bourgogne, XIVe–XVe siècles', in *Inventaires après-décès et ventes de meubles*, Louvain-La-Neuve, 1988, pp. 271–90.

Piponnier, Françoise, 'Le Costume et la mode dans la civilisation médiévale', in *Mensch und Objekt im Mittelalter und in der frühen Neuzeit. Leben, Alltag, Kultur*, (Congress, Krems 1988), Vienna, 1990, pp. 365–96.

Piponnier, Françoise, 'Les Étoffes de deuil', in *À réveiller les morts*, Lyons, P.U.L., 1993, pp. 135–40.

Piponnier, Françoise, 'Étoffes de ville et étoffes de cour', in *La Ville et la cour*, ed. Daniela Romagnoli, Paris, Fayard, 1995, pp. 161–83.

Post, Paul, *Die französisch-niederländische Männetracht einschliesslich der Ritterrüstung im Zeitalter der Spätgotik (1350–1475)*, Halle a. d. Saale, 1910.

Power, Eileen, *The Wool Trade in English Medieval History*, London-New York, Oxford University Press, 1941 (new edn, New York, Greenwood Press, 1987).

Prato, Colloque de l'Istituto internazionale di Storia economica F. Datini (1969): La lana come materia prima, Florence, Leo S. Olschki, 1974.

Prato, Colloque de l'Istituto internazionale di Storia economica F. Datini (1970): Produzione, commercio e consumo dei panni di lana, Florence, Leo S. Olschki, 1976.

Prato, Colloque de l'Istituto internazionale di Storia economica F. Datini (1992): La seta in Europa (sec. XIII–XX), Florence, Le Monnier, 1993.

Quicherat, Jules, *Histoire du costume en France depuis les temps les plus reculés jusqu'à la fin du XVIIIe siècle*, Paris, Hachette, 1877.

Richard, Jules Marie, *Une petite nièce de Saint Louis, Mahaut comtesse d'Artois et de Bourgogne (1302–1329)*, Paris, H. Champion, 1887.

Riché, Pierre and Alexandre-Bidon, Danièle, *L'Enfance au Moyen Âge*, Paris, Le Seuil et Bibliothèque nationale de France, 1994.

Rossiaud, Jacques, *La Prostitution médiévale*, Paris, Flammarion, 1988.

Rubens, Alfred, *A History of Jewish Costume*, London, Weidenfeld & Nicolson, 1967.

Schmitt, Jean-Claude, 'Les Masques, le diable, les morts dans l'Occident médiéval', in *Razo*, 6, Nice, University of Nice, 1986, pp. 87–119.

Scott, M., *The History of Dress Series: Late Gothic Europe 1400–1500*, London, Mills and Boon Ltd, 1980.

Scott, M., *A Visual History of Costume: The Fourteenth and Fifteenth Centuries*, London, Batsford, 1986.

Sicille (Héraut d'Alphonse V, roi d'Aragon), *Le Blason des couleurs en armes, livrées et devises*, Paris, Cocheris, 1857.

Sronkovà, Olga, *Gothic Woman's Fashion*, Prague, Artia, 1954.

Stanilaud, K., *Medieval Craftsmen; Embroiderers,* London, British Museum Press, 1991.

Studies in Honour of Donald King, Textile History, 20, 1989.

Symbole des Alltags, Alltag der Symbole. Mélanges Harry Kühnel, Graz, Akademische Druck und Verlagsantalt, 1992.

Terminologie und Typologie mittelalterlicher Sachgüte: das Beispiel der Kleidung, Vienna, Österreichischen Akademie der Wissenschaften, 1988.

Textile History, Westbury, 1968–.

Thiel, Erika, *Geschichte des Kostüm: die europäische Mode von den Anfängen bis zu Gegenwart*, Wilhelmshafen, Heinrichschafen, 1982.

Thordeman, Bengt, *Armour from the Battle of Wisby 1361*, Stockholm, Almqvist och Wiksell, 2 vols, 1939–40.

Tissu et vêtement: 5000 ans de savoir-faire (exhibition catalogue, Musée archéologique de Guiry-en-Vexin, 25 April–30 November 1986), Guiry-en-Vexin, Musée archéologique, 1986.

Tokui, Yoshiko, 'Usage et symbole du costume de couleur verte dans la France médiévale', *Bulletin de la Société franco-japonaise d'art et d'archéologie*, 6, 1986.

Trichet, Louis, *Le Costume du clergé: ses origines et son évolution en France d'après les règlements de l'Église*, Paris, Du Cerf, 1986.

Turnau, Irena, 'La Bonneterie et l'industrie textile en Europe du XVIᵉ au XVIIIᵉ siècle', *Annales ESC*, 26e année (no. 5), 1971, pp. 1118–32.

Turnau, Irena, *European Occupational Dress*, Warsaw, Académie polonaise des sciences, 1994.

Turska, K., *Ubior dworski w Polce w dobie pierwszych Jagiellonow*, Wroclaw, Polska Akademia Nauk I.H.K.M., 1987.

Vale, Malcolm, *War and Chivalry: Warfare and Aristocratic Cultures in England, France and Burgundy at the End of the Middle Ages*, London, Duckworth, 1981.

Van Thienen, Frithjof W. S., *Huit siècles de costume, l'histoire de la mode en Occident*, Verviers, Gérard & Cie., 1961.

Veale, Elspeth Mary, *The English Fur Trade in the Later Middle Ages*, Oxford, Clarendon Press, 1966.

Le Vêtement, Histoire, archéologie et symbolique vestimentaires au Moyen Âge, Paris, Cahiers du Léopard d'Or, no. 1, 1989.

Wilska, Malgorzata, 'Le Fou de cour: sa place dans la culture médiévale polonaise', *Revue de la Bibliothèque nationale*, 42, 1991, pp. 2–9.

Zangger, Kurt, *Contribution à la terminologie des tissus en ancien français attestés dans des textes français provençaux, italiens, espagnols, allemands et latins*, Zurich, Arts Graphiques Schüler, 1945.

Zeitschrift der Gesellschaft für historische Waffenm-und Kostümkunde, Munich, 1959–.

This book has profited also from the as yet unpublished research of Dominique Cardon, Sophie Desrosiers, Frédérique Lachaud, Boris Lopatinski and Thomas Luttenberg, presented in the seminars on 'Textiles in Medieval Civilisation' at the Ecole des Hautes Etudes en Science Sociales, Paris.

Glossary

AGLET/AIGLET/AIGULLETTE: lacing used to join or fasten items of clothing or armour. Made of leather, or plaited or braided fabric, each aglet has a small metal tag at the end.

ALB: ecclesiastical vestment; full-length white linen tunic, girdled with a cord and often embroidered on the front and around the hem.

ALMUCE: headdress in the shape of a long hood, lined with fur; worn originally by the laity of both sexes and later exclusively by clerics.

AMICE: ecclesiastical vestment; a rectangular piece of fabric, often embroidered, worn round the neck by the priest, under the chasuble.

BALZO: Italian term for a spherical headdress worn by women in northern Italy in the early fifteenth century.

BARDOCUCULLUS: Gallo-Roman garment consisting of hooded cape.

BEIGE: undyed woollen fabric of homespun quality.

BELTS: at the end of the fourteenth century belts could consist of a series of gold or silver panels joined together. They normally consisted, however, of a long strip of fabric or leather with a metal buckle at one end and a matching clasp at the other. A belt would sometimes be decorated with ornamental nails from one end to the other.

BERETTA/BIRETTA: man or woman's headdress; rounded or semi-conical cap fitting closely to the edges; clerical wear by the sixteenth century.

BOURRELET: padded roll or circlet worn by children to protect their heads, or, in the fifteenth century, by men to give volume to their hoods. Also the padded roll added to women's headdresses.

BRAIES: thick linen drawers inherited from the Gauls and worn later by peasants and labourers; the word was also used for smaller garments worn next to the skin.

BRASSARD: a piece of armour worn on the arm.

BRIGANDINE: a suit of armour worn to protect the upper body and hips, composed of strips of steel fixed horizontally to a leather tunic and generally covered with fabric or soft leather.

BROIGNE: body armour covering the whole body and consisting of a leather tunic reinforced with metal plates.

BRUNETTE: good quality woollen fabric, dark brown in colour.

CAFTAN: a gown worn by men; full-length and buttoned down the front, it originated in the Middle East.

CAMELIN: woollen fabric of medium quality, made from camel's hair.

CAUL: coif or tight-fitting cap, fastened under the chin with a knot; worn by men.

CHAPERON: hood, originally covering the head and shoulders. A hole was cut in the fabric to frame the face. The point of the hood was often very long. In the fifteenth century changing masculine fashion dictated that the head should go right through the visor and the neckpiece be raised to form a crest on the head, often on a padded ring (*bourrelet*). The point of the hood was then worn round the neck or round the head.

CHASUBLE: ecclesiastical vestment, sleeveless and circular in cut. Worn by priests over an alb and by bishops over a dalmatic, the chasuble had a hole in the centre for the head to pass through.

CHRISMAL: piece of linen used for enfolding an infant after the ceremony of baptism.

COTE/COTTE: a dress worn over a chemise both by men and women, normally ankle-length and with long tight sleeves. Worn under a surcoat.

COUVRE-CHEF: French term for headgear, current at the end of the Middle Ages to designate the square of fabric worn by peasant women draped in various ways over the head; men wore it at night as a nightcap. A kerchief.

COWL: monastic vestment; hooded mantle.

CREST: collection of decorative items fixed to the top of a helmet; the design of the crest might be heraldic or emblematic in inspiration, or purely invented.

CUIRASS: chest guard of plate-armour made of two rigid pieces, one covering the front and one the back.

CUISSES: armoured thigh guards.

DALMATIC: ecclesiastical vestment worn as an overgarment by a dean, and under his chasuble by a bishop; in shape the dalmatic is a short-sleeved tunic with slits on either side. Worn over the alb.

DEMI-BELT: a variation on the belt worn by women in the fifteenth century. The back part consisted of a leather or fabric band, the front of two chains one with a hook on the end, the other with a clasp or hook.

DEVICE: a phrase containing a thought, an emotion or a command, or, by extension, the badge or emblem accompanying such a phrase.

DOUBLET: item of male clothing, fitted and covering the upper part of the body and hips; originally it was made of several thicknesses of cloth padded with silk or cotton and quilted. It began as an undergarment but gradually came to be worn on its own, with hose.

FIBULA: a clasp or brooch.

FRIEZE: coarse woollen fabric.

FUSAROLE: a disc-shaped or conical object with a central hole, used on the spindle to control the twist applied by the person spinning. Usually made of terra cotta.

FUSTIAN: cotton or linen fabric, or a mixture of the two, usually a cross-weave.

GAMBESON: garment covering the upper part of the body and hips and consisting of several layers of wadding; it was originally padded with hemp, which was held in place by several rows of stitching.

GARLAND: headdress shaped like a coronet, made of fabric or gold or silver.

GAUNTLETS: armoured hand guards or gloves.

GREAVES: armoured shin guards.

HAINCELIN: short *houppelande*, named after Haincelin Coq, court jester to Charles VI of France (1368–1422).

HARNESS: as applied to military equipment, a term for the various parts of the full armour, especially that of armed horsemen (for both man and horse).

HAUBERK: piece of armour made of fine mail that originally covered the head, neck and shoulders.

HELMET: defensive covering for the head; used originally in battle, later only for jousting.

HEUQUE/HUQUE: a sleeveless gown or over-garment, open at the sides.

HOUCE/HOUSSE: one of the garments combining to make up a suit; it had winged sleeves and tabs at the neckline.

HOUPPELANDE: a type of full greatcoat with voluminous sleeves. That worn by men could be either full-length or knee-length and was open down the front. The style for women was always full-length and closed down the front; it sometimes had a train behind. See also ROBE.

HOUSEAUX: high thigh boots.

JAQUE: a short, fitted jerkin, longer than a DOUBLET, reaching to the middle of the thigh or just above the knee, and buttoned in front.

JACK: male outer garment consisting of a fitted bodice with a small skirt.

JAZERANT/JESSERANT: plate armour covering the upper part of the body and hips; the pieces were attached to each other with mail. The word is derived from the Arabic for Algiers (Al-Jezair).

JOURNADE: a full-skirted gown worn by men. It was open under the arms, buttoned at the neck and sometimes bore an armorial device when worn at tournaments.

KERMES SEED: eggs of the insect *kermes vermilio*, which lives on a variety of Mediterranean oak; the eggs were collected before they hatched and crushed to make a very costly red dye, reserved for luxury clothing.

LIVERY: a term originally applied to the seasonal distribution of food and clothes by a prince or nobleman to his retinue. By the end of the fifteenth century, the term was more specifically applied to clothing distributed to the retinue. This came to be of a uniform style, sometimes with a distinctive device or emblem, or mi-parti.

MAIL: originally a metal plate fixed on to a soldier's clothing to strengthen it. Chain mail consisted of interlocking metal rings which produced a much more flexible kind of armour.

MANIPLE: ecclesiastical vestment; a straight band of fabric suspended from a priest's left forearm and generally matching his chasuble and stole.

MANTELET/MANTLET: short, full male garment, open on both sides.

MANTLE: loose outer garment or cloak cut in the round, open down the front and fastened either on the shoulder or in front; for men or women.

MITRE: headdress worn by a bishop.

OPUS ANGLICANUM (Lat. English work): type of embroidery originating in England and characterised by an underside couching technique.

ORPHREY: band of silk decorated with embroidery and, sometimes, gold ornamentation. Used to decorate ecclesiastical vestments.

PALETOT: loose, short masculine gown, with short sleeves.

PALL: piece of fabric used during certain church ceremonies: it was held over the bride and bridegroom during a wedding and draped over the coffin during funerals.

PALLIUM: in late Antiquity, a full ecclesiastical cloak which later was reduced to a long band of fabric encircling the priest's shoulders with a panel at the front and back, worn over the chasuble. The pallium ceased to be worn before the end of the Middle Ages. The term has also been applied to a canopy and to any liturgical hanging (see PALL).

PATTENS: footwear consisting of a wooden or cork sole, sometimes in two pieces, and held on by a strap over the instep. Pattens were usually worn over light shoes.

PELISSE/PELISSON/PELIÇON: fur garment, sometimes covered with fabric on the outside; a waistcoat worn under the overcoat. Worn mainly by women of modest means.

PLATES: pieces of iron, often tempered, cut into different shapes by armourers to reinforce the different garments worn for battle.

ROBE: In the fourteenth century, a suit of clothes for men and women, and retained for ceremonial/court wear (*robe royale*) into the fifteenth century. From *c.*1430, the *robe* in France refers to an outer sleeved garment for men and women; the word in English is usually 'gown' in this context.

ROCHET: loose garment made of linen, worn over normal clothing by various different categories of labourers. A protective garment worn also by the clergy from the thirteenth century, which became the prerogative of bishops, cardinals and canons regular.

SACK: a kind of mantle.

SAIE/SAYON: short cape worn by the Franks.

SAMITE: silk fabric with a diagonal weave that makes it look like satin.

SCAPULAR: monastic garment made of a broad band of fabric slit in the middle to accommodate the head, and hanging loosely in front and behind.

SENDAL: a light silk fabric.

SERGE: fabric made of wool or a mixture of wool and cotton; its cross-weave gives it a diagonal or chevroned aspect.

SOLLERETS: pieces of armour designed to protect the feet.

SURCOAT: one of the garments combining to make a ROBE. The open surcoat had very wide sleeves that revealed the COTTA worn underneath and, sometimes, its side lacing.

SURPLICE: fine linen tunic worn over ordinary clothes by members of the clergy in church, when not officiating at a service, or during processions outside. Also a kind of smock worn by the laity (see ROCHET).

TALLIT: originally a ritual cloak worn by Jews, later a rectangular piece of cloth worn at synagogue for prayer or at weddings.

TIARA: ecclesiastical headdress worn by the pope.

TIRETAINE: woollen fabric of mediocre quality.

TOURET: originally a band of fabric worn like a coronet around a woman's veil; later a cylindrical headdress of the same shape.

VISOR: the front piece of the helmets worn during the Hundred Years War; could be either fixed or mobile.

ZIZIYYOT: ritual fringes attached to the edges of the *tallit* worn by Jews at the synagogue.

Photograph Credits

Brussels, Bibliothèque Royale Albert Ier: 25, 28; Cesena, Biblioteca Malatestiana: 47; Chelles, Musée de Chelles/photo: E. Mittard and N. Georgieff: 3; Dijon, Bibliothèque municipale: 44; Florence, Scala: 32, 1; Heidelberg, Universitätsbibliothek: 26, 51; The Hague, Koninklijke Bibliotheek: 9; Lisbon, Arquivo Nacional de Fotografia: 46; London, The British Library: 5, 50; London, The National Gallery: 6; Madrid, El Patrimonio National: 33; Madrid, Oronoz: 54; Munich, Bayerische Staatsbibliothek: 49; New York, The Metropolitan Museum of Art: 17; New York, The Pierpont Morgan Library: 15; New York, Spencer Collection/The New York Public Library/Astor, Lenox and Tilden Foundations: 4; Nuremberg, Stadtbibliothek: 52; Oxford, Bodleian Library, University of Oxford: 58; Paris, Archives nationales: 12; Paris, Archives Photographiques/SPADEM: 8; Paris, Bibliothèque nationale de France: 2, 10, 11, 14, 21, 22, 23, 24, 31, 34, 39, 40, 41, 42, 50, 53, 56, 59, 60; Paris, Réunion des musées nationaux: 37; Poitiers, Musées de Poitiers/photo C. Vignaud: 27; Prague, Narodni Knihovna: 36; Rome, Vatican, Biblioteca Apostolica: 48; Saint-Jean-de-Maurienne, Club Photo du Collège Maurienne: 17; Stuttgart, Württembergische Landesbibliothek: 13; Valenciennes, Bibliothèque municipale/photo La Boîte à Image G.P. Simon: 45; Vanves, Giraudon: 29, 55; Vanves, Lauros-Giraudon: 7, 16, 57; Varsovie, Muzeum Narodowe: 35; Vienna, Oesterreichischen Nationalbibliothek: 18, 20, 38, 43